The Qur'ãnic Cosmology

The Eternal Truth...

The Qur'ãnic Cosmology

The Eternal Truth...

Moid Siddiqui

KITAB BHAVAN
NEW DELHI-110002

Kitab Bhavan
Publishers, Distributors, Exporters & Importers
1784, Kalan Mahal, Darya Ganj
New Delhi-110002 (India)

Phone : (91-11) 23277392/3, 23274686
Fax : (91-11) 23263383
E-mail : nasri@vsnl.com
Web Site: www.kitabbhavan.com

First Edition ... 2004

ISBN : 81-7151-344-1

Laser Typesetting at:
Laser Track
Darya Ganj, New Delhi-110002

Published in India by:
Nusrat Ali Nasri for Kitab Bhavan
1784, Kalan Mahal, Darya Ganj
New Delhi-110002 (India)

Printed in India at:
Nice Printing Press
Khureji Khas, Delhi-110051

DEDICATION

I dedicate this spiritual work to Dr. Naeem Siddiqui, my brother-in-law, who exists forever in our fond memories. He parted us to meet again in the eternal life beyond space and time —hereafter.

I dedicate this 'heart-work' to Naseem, my sister, Nilofar, my niece, Nasser and Naveed, my nephews, praying Allah to rectify their hearts and heal their souls.

I dedicate this lifework to his sisters—Quoresha and Ruquiya—whose soul-testing forbearance is akin to piety.

Moid Siddiqui

CONTENTS

PREFACE

Ask a simple question to anyone: "Do you believe in God?" If the response is in affirmation, his or her belief in oneness of God stands established. How? Read the question carefully.

Even the 'atheists' dispute existence of God in *singular* and never in *plural*. The dispute that atheists raise is, "Whether there is a God or not?" and never, "Whether there are Gods or not?"

Every religion, at its deepness has the seat of onesess of God—you need to scratch a bit and discover. 'One and Only' is an established faith of most of the religions. This oness has now become the focal point of science; the 'string theory' or 'bootstrap theory' on which Stephan Hawking is currently working in this direction.

'Cosmos' is the creation of God, without any partnership. To understand His greatness one has to understand the vastness of Cosmos.Human vocabulary is incapable to describe the glory of God.

For this reason Lao Tzu — the old master (5th century BC) — says, "For lack of words I call Him great!"

I am not the student of Astronomy or Cosmology. It was my urge to understand the kingdom of God that led to this path. In this endeavor I owe a lots to the great works of Albert Einstein, Carl Sagan, Gary Zukav, Stephan Hawking, Fritjof Capra, Maurice Bucaille and lots many. The great works of Dr. Rafiq Zakaria, Maulana Abul Kalam Azad and many other scholars find reflection in this work. I acknowledge my sincere thanks to all of them.

A last word — I have deliberately used 'American spelling' for giving 'Qur'ãnic Cosmology' a corporate flavor.

Moid Siddiqui

ISLAM – AS I UNDERSTAND

A peaceful world with a compassionate heart that beats for universality and humanity is the new dawn that I look for each cockcrow.

In October 1999 I participated in the global convention organized by State of the World Forum at San Francisco on the theme, 'Envisioning and Creating a Sustainable Compassionate Society – A step towards a culture of peace'. In this spiritual convention I got a unique opportunity to share my views. The theme of the 'Roundtable Session' was 'Spirituality and Religion'. I was asked to address a delicate issue, "Each religion is sacred, why then so much bloodshed in the name of religion?"

It was a great challenge and a rare opportunity to me. The theme was very sensitive but exciting. I paused for a while and began. It was perhaps the divine intervention that gave power and clarity to my words. I was aware, there were Christians, Muslims, Hindus, Buddhists, Jains, besides a few spiritual priests and priestesses, and representatives from various spiritual organizations, including Mrs. Nahid Angha, Director, International Association of Sufism.

I began...

"I share with you my personal views; if I am wrong,

I wish to be corrected," was my opening sentence. Then I raised three points as the cause of bloodshed in the name of religion. The language was not as articulated as follows with quotation of Qur'ãnic verses, though:

Firstly, we never see the things with the 'frame of reference' of others' perception. One rejects other without even understanding the basics, let alone grasping the underlying philosophy or fundamental principle. We see the practice of the followers and mistake this as one's religion. The practices followed by the followers of a particular religion may not necessarily be the actual teachings of that religion. The stereotypes block the doorway to understanding. Religion is not always what the followers practise. There ought to be an underlying divinity somewhere in the existing practice or in the 'forgotten' philosophy by the followers. This can be true for a person; this can also be true for a group of persons. This tendency is generic and should not be particularized.

Then I set the pitch of my voice and asked how many of them knew that we the Muslims believe in the Prophet-hood of Christ, Moses, Isaac, Abraham, and many others? How many of them knew that we the Muslims believe in the miraculous birth of Christ; if one does not believe, he is not a Muslim. How many of them knew that we the Muslims believe in the virginity of Mother Marry; if someone refutes, he is not a Muslim. How many of them knew that a true Muslim is supposed to show reverence for and speak not ill about the

Messengers of almighty, born in different nations/races for we know not who is from the blessed group of 124000 prophets came to the Earth prior to Prophet Muhammad. No other person than Prophet Muhammad told himself this to the mankind. If someone does not believe this, he is not a Muslim. How many of them knew that Qur'ãn proclaims: "Remember: To every nation We have sent an apostle for people to be rightly guided."

Then I asked the Hindu brethren, how many of them were aware of the Ashlok – 'Ekko Brahamam, Dutyia Nahisti' meaning 'God is one and only and there is none, besides Him'.

There was a lull! I paused for a while and continued.

Secondly, each of us claims to know one's own religion but, really, knows not in most of the cases. Mostly the superficiality is misunderstood as in-depth knowledge about one's religion. Our position is like Newton's boy who is playing on the seashore, and collecting a few pebbles or prettier shells with a feeling of greatness, while the great ocean of truth watches still and calm. How much ignorant we are about our own respective religions!

I asked, whether my Buddhist brethren knew the message given by Buddha to his followers: 'When you see Buddha on the road, kill him', which means follow what Buddha said but don't mistake to believe him as ultimate reality. Whether Buddhist knew what Buddha told at his last hour to his disciples? He said, "See that you do not worship my ashes. If you do, the path of salvation will be closed to you."

I paused for picking up appropriate words...

Islam is misunderstood not only by non-Muslims but also by some of Muslims. It is a simple religion of universality and humanism. It is a peaceful and impartial religion as I understand; if I am wrong I wish to be corrected. Allah is 'Rabbil Aalameen' (The Lord of Universes) and His domain should not be marginalized considering Him only as 'Rabbil Muslimeen'. Muslims, His servants, must be humane to the entire humanity without any distinction on the basis of colour, race, caste and creed believing in universality of Islam.

I looked at Mrs. Nahid Angha, and asked how many Muslims believe and hold faith steadfast that there was no land to which God had not sent His messengers? Then, I clarified what I meant by 'firm faith'. 'Reading cursorily' is not 'understanding'; 'Understanding superficially' is not 'believing'; 'Believing halfheartedly' is not 'faith'. Did Allah not mention in Qur'ãn, 'We did aforetime send Messengers before thee...' (Ghafir— 40:78) and made it clear to mankind in the same *Surah* 'Some We have mentioned to you, and others We have not.' Are we not supposed to be humble to ancient people of wisdom for we know not their identity? Qur'ãn indicated only 28 of them; 14 clearly and 14 casually.

Again there was silence. I modulated my voice and concluded making the third point.

More than 80% of world's population believes in God. It is only less than 20% who are either atheists or do not follow any religion. I am not aware of any bloodshed between these two lots of 80% and 20%. Humankind has witnessed the bloodshed in the name of religions only among the lot of 80% – the segment that believe in existence of God.

I read the faces and entered the most crucial phase of my observation on 'why bloodshed is there in the name of religions?' I was weighing the words carefully, lest my perception succumbs to superficial vocabulary or unintended meaning which any man of language could impose on me, giving a meaning to my words diagonally opposite to what I intended. Most of the time we catch the words and split the hair rather trying to understand the 'intent'. What we fail to understand that sometimes the 'intent' is beyond expression through the mode of language.

There was an inquiring silence and inviting expressions on the faces…

The difference among this lot of 80% is broadly in understanding the 'Attributes' of God and not in accepting or denying the existence of God.

If people of each faith just count upon the 'commonalties' and keep them in sharp focus, better understanding and wisdom will prevail.

But, unfortunately I understand not fully my own religion; I do not try to understand fully other's religion, yet I want him to follow me. And unfortunately he understands not his religion; he understands not others' religion, yet he wants me to follow him.

Then, I described what *Surah Kaferoon* teaches us:

"Proclaim! Listen ye who disbelieve! I worship not that which ye worship, nor do ye worship that which I worship. And I shall not worship that which ye worship, nor will you worship that which I worship. Unto you is your religion, and unto me is my religion." If all of us follow this Qur'ãnic ordain in true spirit, there cannot be any bloodshed in the name of religion.

Let each of us understand fully one's own religion first.

Silence of sphinx; I held my breath.

The thin pause broke with claps.

Now when I am writing 'Qur'ãnic Cosmology' with the understanding of Qur'ãn and Astronomy, I repeat once again the same words with the same humility: "It is my understanding of Islam; if I am wrong, I wish to be corrected. It is my understanding of Astronomy; if I am wrong, I wish to be corrected."

I am neither a physicist nor a cosmologist. But today such monopoly is not accepted nor does such monopoly exist. Corporate World knows how Gary Zukav acquired the knowledge of physics and wrote the prize-winning book 'The Dancing Wu Li Masters' and later 'The Seat of the Soul'. I read many books on cosmology and astronomy with purity in mind to understand the vastness of kingdom of God. This book is the reflection of what I could gather.

As regards my understanding of Islam and Qur'ãn, my searching inquiries are the source that gives clarity and support to my understanding Islam with the perspective of its universality and humanism. It is my understanding after a painstaking quest through my intuitive wisdom and insightful learning. If I have erred in understanding, I wish to be guided and corrected.

To my mind, most of the time the cause of variance in understanding others' perspective lies in human factor. Sometimes the variance takes place while putting the ultimate truth in words in different languages, as each language stands distinct with its own dialect and metaphor. Obviously, sometimes the interpretation may differ from person to person. One may interpret it differently, with the application of one's feeble brain through imperfect perceptions.

The human factor whenever entered the religion, it corrupted truth. Since time immemorial this has been happening and the future would witness no other newer experience. The human brain cannot comprehend the truth of wholeness easily. "Tao that can be told is not Tao", said the Old Master, Lao Tzu 2500 years ago. One needs to comprehend It through one's intuitive mind. It is not enough to say 'God is there.'

Each one of us should have the inquisitive craving to discover Him.

Most of us fail to grasp human philosophy and human thoughts of philosophers and monks like Socrates, Aristotle, Plato, Confucius, Lao Tzu, Buddha, Durkheim, St. Paul, Hegel, Karl Marx, Kahlil Gibran, Rumi, and scores and scores of them. The supreme truth is subtle; it needs prudence for comprehension. Understanding of spirituality warrants much deeper insight and intuitive wisdom. A mind with searching enquiries and a heart filled with purity, compassion, and love can take you there. 'Feelings' is the language of soul. One must hear the whispers when Life talks to you.

My understanding of cosmic truth does not stand in isolation. It stays in togetherness. Truth is cosmic; it came unto humankind again and again. One needs to develop the intuitive eye to see the invisible, and the divine wisdom to understand the divinity.

Every soul is potentially divine, said Swami Vivekananda. The Holy Scriptures (in their original form) ought to be filled with spirituality describing the same Cosmic Truth in different languages with different dialect and slang, is my understanding. How one picks up the truth is one's divine ability.

Every soul is pure. It ought to be. People of faith must know and remember what God proclaims in Qur'ãn: "When I have fashioned him (in due proportion) and breathed into him (Adam) of My spirit..."

(Al-Hijr—15:29). As per Islam, each of us descended from the heritage of Adam. Adam, whom God fashioned in due proportion and breathed into him of His spirit. That Cosmic breath is filled in each of us what we call Soul. Therefore, each human soul is ought to be pure. Our wrong doings and sins make it impure and then, the soul requires healing. It is so simple to understand, so difficult to be certain of!

Life is not a physical journey. We often mix up our physical self, intellectual self and psychic with our spiritual self and take them as one and the same. When I say 'divine soul' I mean the spiritual self, not the physical or psychic, or intellectual self. I want to make it loud and clear lest I am taken wrong.

'How many of us have tried to understand humanity from this angle?' is a question that should ring loud bells in each mind, if our intellect is alive and vibrant. Today, having made a humble study of various books on 'spirituality, I understand why the ancient Sufis and Saints said: 'The 'Killer' and the 'Killed' are same!' Meaning, both have the same divine soul. 'Killing' is a physical action; soul has no role to play. To understand spirituality one must learn to understand 'paradoxes' first. One must try to get on a higher plane beyond five sensory perceptions. One needs to become a multi-sensory perceptive person. Simple to say, difficult to acquire!

·Fountainhead...

The basic thing that we forget quite conveniently is

that the source of each of us is same. The fountainhead – the creator – is the same God, call Him and remember Him with any name or imagination. When water flows from the fountainhead, it may take many streams. Each stream may pass through different pastures and pieces of land, with different hygienic conditions. The flow of each stream may not be the same; the colour and purity of water may also differ. But this does not take away the stream from the fountainhead. It just cannot separate from the fountainhead.

Those with narrow vision and shallow knowledge only try to pick up the holes and malice every such attempt which is made today to bring the 'commonalties' of various religions into sharp focus. What we forget is that we belong to one common source and the basic belief in God ought to be same; the difference that occurs is due to human factor.

Human factor, human factor, human factor... The cause in variance I attribute to human factor. I would say this until my tongue bleeds.

God confirms in Qur'ān:

"Men were at first of one religion only;

Then they fell to variance." (Yunus—10:19)

"Mankind were of one nation, and God sent prophets as bringer of glad-Tiding and Warners and He sent down with them the word of Truth that it might decide the disputes of men." (Al-baqrah—2:213)

"And we have already sent apostles before thee;

of some We have told thee, and of others We have told thee nothing." (Ghafir—40:78)

Professor Rafiqu Zakaria in his famous book, 'Muhammad and Qur'ãn' describes about the prophets from Adam to Christ vis-à-vis Qur'ãnic revelations. "The stories of the prophets who had preceded Muhammad account for almost a quarter of Qur'ãn; they number twenty eight in all. The list of twenty eight in all, however, by no means exhaustive." He then quotes from Qur'ãn, "Some We have mentioned to you, and some others We have not." He proceeds, "The Qur'ãn contains another verse to the effect that there was no land to which God had not sent His messengers. These messengers had revealed the Truth to their people in their respective languages. Their accounts form part of the Qur'ãn... (Hud—11:120-123)"

And Maulana Abdullah Yusuf Ali clarifies: "God sent some messengers of Truth to every people. There are some whose names are known to us through the Holy Qur'ãn, but there are a large number whose names are not made known to us through that medium. We must recognise the Truth wherever we find it."

Similar wisdom came to me from the writings of another Islamic Scholar – Maulana Abul Kalam Azad. "The Din," observes Maulana, "as the Qur'ãn asserts, was given to every community or section of mankind through chosen men called Prophets. Every religion in existence today was at first, at its base, nothing but this Din which the Qur'ãn speaks of, delivered through every Prophet and embodied in every scripture."

It is time to bring about peace on this planet where humanity dwells. Only understanding each religion in right perspective, breaking the man-made hard shell can bring about such universal peace. Every religion tried to break the shell but the followers made it hardened.

"Say: We believe in God, and in what hath been sent down to us, and what hath been sent down to Abraham, and Ishmael and Isaac, and Jacob, and the tribes, and in (the books) given to Moses, Jesus, and the Prophets from their Lord. We make no difference between them. And to Him are we submitted (in Islam)." (Aal-Imran—3:84)

I once again intellectualize support from the thoughts of Maulana Azad from his 'Basic concepts of Qur'ãn'. I admire his confidence and clarity of thought. It really calls for an in-depth knowledge and insight of Qur'ãn to make such a powerful statement as under:

"The expression 'We make no difference between them' in the above verse recurs in various places in the Qur'ãn just to mark its disapproval of the tendency of regarding one prophet and rejecting to another, or of accepting one prophet as superior to another, or of accepting one prophet and rejecting another as bearer of truth. Qur'ãn calls upon everyone who cares to follow the way laid down by God to accept without discrimination all the prophets and the scriptures revealed to them and the basic truth which they all contain, and to accept it wherever found and in whatever language expressed..."

My understanding of Qur'ãn comes from the underlying universality that was revealed unto us again and again. Qur'ãn – the Holy Scripture of sixth century AD – reveals unto us the cosmic truth. The cosmic truth came from God earlier to Qur'ãn as well, in every epoch, to the humankind at every patch of Earth. Qur'ãn makes it clear that to every land throughout history of mankind, God sent his messengers:

> Remember: To every nation
>
> We have sent an apostle
>
> For people to be rightly guided... (Yunus—10:47)
>
> 'Among the apostles, make no distinction...'
>
> (Al-Baqrah—2:285)

As mentioned earlier, according to a saying of Prophet Muhammad (peace be upon him), God had sent 1,24,000 messengers – they were like 'needles in the comb'. Some of them are mentioned in the Qur'ãn, many are not. Qur'ãn indicates that there was no land to which God had not sent His messengers. These messengers had revealed the truth to their people probably in their respective languages. Obviously, the language of revelations could be Arabic, Hebrew, or who knows, could be Mandarin, Sanskrit or Latin, and so on. To quote Maulana Azad:

"...The divine truth, says Qur'ãn, is a universal gift from God. It is not exclusive to any race or any people or religious group and is not exclusively delivered in any particular language..."

"...The Qur'ãn has repeatedly pronounced that discrimination between prophets amounts to a denial of the Din of God itself which recognizes them all without discrimination. There are therefore only but two ways open for man. One is the way of recognition of them all; the other is that of rejection. There is no third one. The rejection of even one prophet means the rejection of every other as well."

Maulana then quotes another Qur'ãnic verse to bring home the understanding about the universality of Qur'ãn:

"Of a truth they who believe not in God and His apostles, and seek to separate God from His apostles, and say 'some we believe and some we believe not', and desire to take a middle course: These! They are veritable disbelievers ..." (An-Nisa—4:149)

Maulana further guides us:

"Qur'ãn calls upon man to believe in God and practice righteous living in conformity with that belief and not to condemn anybody's religion or reject its founder. It says that it confirms the basic message common to all religions and endorses it as its own message. When such is the Qur'ãnic attitude, why, asks the Qur'ãn, do the followers of other religions declare war against the Qur'ãn?

...The primary aim of this spiritual law of life or the way of God, the Din, was to keep mankind united and not to serve as a force of disunity."

Qur'ãn stands for unity and not disunity. The almighty makes this loud and clear unto us in Surah Al-Hujarat, verse 13:

O mankind! We created you from a single (pair) of a male and a female, and made you into nations and tribes, that ye may know each other (not that ye may despise each other).

To my mind, Qur'ãn casts an obligation on each of us not only simply to know our 'single source' of origin, but also to work towards bringing about unity and harmony among humankind. Again, yet another obligation cast upon us is to make conscious efforts against the forces that may cause disunity in the humankind. Both stand complementary as two faces of the same coin. Bear in mind the objective mentioned in Qur'ãn; the divine purpose of division into tribes, race and nations was 'that you may know each other, not that you may despise each other'.

This message of oneness of humankind has come to mankind from time immemorial. 'Vasudaiva Kutumbam' is the phrase used in Hindu Scripture in the BC era that stands to proclaim, 'World a single family'.

To understand the factors that stand for 'variations' in understanding the divine truth, it is necessary to understand the time factor to get better clarity.

Islam through Qur'ãn came to humankind when documentation was not a difficult process. It was the great advantageous factor in freezing the revelations in the form as they were revealed. The messages of God that came earlier again and again lacked this advantage. The other most important and rather the divine favour to Qur'ãn is that Allah has taken the responsibility to preserve its purity in His divine custody where no human factor can enter:

'We have, without doubt, sent down message: and We will assuredly guard it (from corruption)'

Bible – Old Testament and New Testament – as available to us was written 'under the guidance of God...', as Columbia encyclopedia puts it. Obviously, presence of human factor can not be ruled out for the text that is available in the form today! Perhaps, this human factor could be the cause of different interpretation by Protestants and Roman Catholics – the latter does not give right to any individual to interpret Bible and insists to follow the interpretation made by the Church. The Old Testament was in Hebrew and the New Testament came to us in Greek. Any version in English cannot be original at first place.

The first translation of whole Bible was Latin Vulgate of St. Jerome. The Columbia Encyclopedia flowcharts the history of Bible as follows:

English Bible of John (1384); The first printed English translation of New Testament English by William Tyndale (1525-26); then by Miles Coverdale (1535);

the Authorized Version (AV), known as King James version (KJV) was published in 1611. In the 19th century, the Authorized Version was revised as English Revised Version and American Revised Version (1880-90)... American scholars published (1952) the Influential Revised Standard Version (RSV). An English translation of French Catholic Bible 'de Jerusalem' appeared as 'Jerusalem Bible' in 1966. The new translations are the New English Bible, Westminster Version, and New American Bible (1970).

How the original message of God to Moses and Christ can be perceived in its original form is more a matter of choice – have your pick!

It is a common knowledge and understanding amongst Muslims that before Qur'ãn Allah had revealed unto mankind through Torah, Zabur, and Bible. We always refer only these four revelations. But to my understanding from Qur'ãn, His revelations were beyond this:

"Say: We believe in God, and in what hath been sent down to us, and what hath been sent down to Abraham, and Ishmael and Isaac, and Jacob, and the tribes, and in (the books) given to Moses, Jesus, and the Prophets from their Lord. We make no difference between them. And to Him are we resigned."
(Aal-Imran—3:84)

'To you (Prophet Muhammad) hath He presented the faith which we commanded unto Noah, and which we have revealed to thee, and which we commanded unto Abraham and Mosses and Jesus, saying, "Observe this faith, and be not divided into sects therein"

'Verily We have revealed to thee as We revealed to Noah and the prophets after him, and as We reveled to Abraham, and Ishmael, and Isaac, and Jacob, and the tribes and Jesus, and Job and Jonah, Aaron, and Solomon; and to David We gave psalms. Of some apostles We have told thee before; of other apostles We have not told thee – Apostles charged to announce and to warn, that men, after those apostles, might have no plea against God.' (An-Nisa—4: 163-164)

Revelations of God came to prophets besides the Holy Scriptures mostly quoted only as Qur'ān (revealed to Prophet Muhammad), Injeel (Bible – Prophet Jesus Christ), Zabur (Psalms bestowed upon Prophet David) Torait (Torah – the revelations came to Prophet Moses).

Others before Prophet Muhammad (peace be upon him) had born beyond the reach of history. Prophet Muhammad came in the fullest blaze of history. He walked upright and straight.

'We have sent these inspiration, as We sent it to Noah and the Messengers after him...

(An-Nisa—4:163)

In Tafseer, Abdullah Yusuf Ali elaborates, "First we have a general statement: that inspiration was sent to many Messengers, and the inspiration was of the same kind as that sent to the Prophet Muhammad, for Allah's message is one. Note that what is spoken of here is 'inspiration', not necessarily of Book. Every nation or group of people had a messenger: (Yunus—10:47). Some of these messengers have been mentioned by name in the Qur'ãn, and some not (An-Nisa—4:164)"

What was revealed unto Noah, Abraham, Ishmael, Isaac, Jacob, and the tribes and to many other prophets from the Lord is not with us in a documented or verbal form. We are also not aware of the languages in which those revelations were sent. This does not give us the liberty to interpret the truth in any other way than as revealed to us in Qur'ãn:

'Say: Will ye dispute with us about God when He is our Lord and your Lord? We have result of our deeds and ye have the result of your deeds, and we are sincerely His.'

The message of God through Qur'ãn is unambiguous... 'We have the result of our deeds and you have the result of your deeds...' 'And surely Allah is my Lord and your Lord. So serve him' (Maryam—19:37)

Then, 'Why so much bloodshed in the name of religions?' The question that was asked in the global seminar haunts me. This sets the urge for searching inquiries.

An incident that solves the riddle to some extent...

It was a Delta Airline's flight bound to New York, that I boarded from Bombay in October 1999. At Frankfurt a new passenger occupied my neighboring seat. I was tired; I sank in my seat and didn't look at him. I heard the airhostess whispering to me, "Hindu

Vegetarian Meals?" and I nodded my head confirming 'Yes'. I avoid non-vegetarian food where I am not sure of 'Halal' food. Peculiarly, the vegetarian food is booked as 'Hindu Vegetarian Meals' in international flights in Western airlines. She served the supper to me and to my co-passenger – it was non-vegetarian food for him – some pieces of roasted lamb, sausages, loafs and salad... He requested for vegetarian food. The airhostess apologized for there was no such advance choice booking by him. He returned the tray and asked for some biscuits or bread loafs. For sure, he was a Jew I could make out. Being a Jew he was not supposed to take non-vegetarian food without performing 'Kosher'.

I started my 'Hindu' vegetarian meals. He was swallowing the leafs of salad and biting the pieces of loaf and biscuits served as courtesy by the airhostess. He started the dialogue first.

"From India?"

"Yes," I said.

"Enjoying Hindu vegetarian meals?"

"Yes." I smiled in response.

"Must have booked in advance?" He made an enquiry and I confirmed it once again with my brief answer "Yes." But he continued...

"I have visited India many times. I know you Hindus are very particular for vegetarian diet." I was not surprised. I was taking the 'Hindu' vegetarian food and anyone else would have made a similar guess about my religion identity. I responded with a smile and asked why didn't he take the roasted pieces of lamb?

"I do not take lamb, beef or chicken while touring," was his simple reply. He thought why to exert in explaining what I would not understand; as per his understanding I was a Hindu, taking a 'Hindu vegetarian' food. I decided to be a bit mischievous to him, as he was not coming out openly, Why didn't he take the lamb?"

"Is it not because you are not sure whether 'Kosher' is performed while cutting the lamb?" My pointblank unexpected question gave a whack on his head. He was perhaps thinking, 'How the hell this guy knows so much about 'Kosher!' I continued, "I understand you perform 'Kosher' as Muslims do 'Halal'?" He agreed but frowned at me. He was not very happy being compared with a Muslim practice, I could read this clearly on his face. He looked at me with an eagle eye. Who is this guy? I was coolly taking my 'Hindu' meals. Obviously, I was a Hindu in his understanding.

After some time he became quite friendly with me. He was praising Hindus and simultaneously he was highly critic about 'Moslems'. He had gone to the extent of suggesting to me, 'never believe a Moslem'. It was the real test of my patience, but as a corporate guy I know when to drop the curtain, when not to... I continued without disclosing my identity. Perhaps a bigger purpose was to be achieved by me as willed by God.

I continued discussing about religion and found that he was very strong in history of various religions, especially Judaism, Christianity and Islam. He was critical against Islam giving an impression as if it was just contradictory to the faith of Jews'. But when it came to Christianity, he clarified to me that basically there was no conflict of thought or faith between Jews and Christians. "We believe in Old Testament, they believe in New Testament. The Bible is same..."

"Then, what is Torah?" I enquired. Before he could say, I explained, "Torah was revealed unto Moses. What Christians relate to Christ is Gospel, rather Bible. Bible covers a larger gamut than what revealed to Christ. It covers even the psalms revealed unto David." I paused for a while and looked into his eyes. He was keenly listening to me. "I understand, Qur'ãn makes reference about these Psalms which came as an enlightenment to David, whom Moslems call Prophet Daud..." During discussions he admired that being a Hindu (in his understanding) I knew so much about Judaism, Christianity and Islam. I smiled. I was aiming at larger purpose. I made a polite query.

"Since Bible is embodiment of 'Old Testament' and 'New Testament', you believe Judaism and Christianity co-exist and very similar, and Islam is just diagonally opposite to your faith?"

"Yes." He confirmed.

"Oh! I see." I paused to pick the right words. "You are so confident. Obviously, you must have read Qur'ãn and found a gross difference between your religion and Islamic faith." I threw a spaghetti that would surely stick and it stuck.

"No, I have never read Qur'ãn. Why should I ..."

"So, it is an assumption by you that both these faiths – Islam and Judaism – are diagonally opposite. You said Judaism and Christianity co-exist, then why didn't you take lamb, cut, cooked and served by Christians?" I asked setting innocence on my face.

"No, I am not supposed to take non-vegetarian food served by Christians.

"Why? Do they not perform 'Kosher' like Jews or 'Halal' like Moslems?" I fired another innocent query and the fellow really got the shock of his life. But he had no option than to say the truth. "Yes, they don't perform 'Kosher' or 'Halal' as Jews and Moslems do." One can imagine my excitement.

"It means there is more resemblance in performing 'Kosher' between Jews and Muslims. But you told me that Muslims' faith is totally opposite to Jews' faith."

"May be," he paused. "May be there is some likeness between Jews and Moslems. May be... But their faith clashes grossly with our faith." He maintained his stand and I decided to keep cool using my patience and intuitive wisdom that was leading me to the path perhaps willed by Allah.

"Oh, I see," I gave an impression agreeing with him but in the same breath I threw another bombshell. "What about 'circumcision'? "Do Jews follow it?"

"Yes."

Do Christians follow it?"

"No."

"What do you think, whether Moslems follow 'circumcision'?"

"Yes, I understand Moslems follow this practice." He was almost fumbling.

"How's that the practice started at Noah's time was followed by the people of faith of Moses, and Prophet Muhammad, was later discarded by Christians? Obviously, Christ must have born after Prophet Muhammad?" Wittingly I made a query with a purpose in mind building a logical sequence.

"Certainly not," he jumped in his seat. He was a bit comfortable with my 'lack of knowledge'. "Christ was born almost 600 years before Muhammad was born."

"Then I am a bit confused," I pretended. "Please correct me if I am getting you wrong... It means what practised by people before Moses, then by Moses' followers was discarded by Christians but again re-adopted by Muslims as per Islamic faith. Then how's that you say the faith and practices of Jews and Christians are similar and diagonally opposite with Moslems'?" I was looking straight into his eyes, and I could see the discomfort on his face and assess the embarrassment that he was passing through.

There was a lull. He unchoked his throat and told. "What you say makes some sense to me; yes 'circumcision' is commonly followed by Jews and Moslems; Christians do not believe and do not follow circumcision. Yes, it means what stopped by Christians was renewed by Muhammad...."

"Meaning that there is more similarity in the faiths of Jews and Muslims?" I was excited and asked this question hurriedly thinking that my purpose was served and he would give up.

"No," was his firm reply. It is just one similarity between Jewish and Mohammedan faith. We don't agree with each other, as there is a basic difference in our faiths..."

"Not just one," I corrected him. "Just now I learnt from you that Muslims also follow Halal as you follow 'Kosher', but Christians do not believe in Halal or Kosher..."

"Yes, I agree." I found he was quite honest and logical. He surrendered without taking a hard position.

Then we chatted on various interesting issues on culture, civilization and slowly I brought him back to Judaism and Islam.

"I understand Muslims do not perform 'Halal' on fish or other seafood. Do you perform Kosher on fish?"

"No we too do not perform 'Kosher' on fish or other seafood..."

"Oh Gosh! One more similarity..." I exaggerated my excitement.

"No... There is a difference." He stopped me. "Unless it is confirmed to us by another Jew that fish had not died in the water, we are not supposed to take fish..."

"Wonderful!" This was my turn to stop him before he finished his sentence. "The same reason was explained to me by one of my Muslim friends. It appears, Muslims are not supposed to take a dead fish in water. Amazing! Isn't amazing?" I looked at him and he didn't know how to respond. He went half way with my excitement smiling together with me then whispered, "Are you sure, Moslems do not take fish died in water?" And I confirmed repeating that one staunch Muslim friend gave precisely the same version to me.

"So one more likeness among two faiths! Isn't it?"

"Yes... Yes..." He agreed with me forcing a smile on his face to match mine.

"Oh! I forgot to ask one thing. Does Torah permit you to eat ham – the meat of swine?"

"No," was his firm reply.

"Does Old Testament mention any where 'pig' in the list of permissible animals which can be eaten?"

"No, on contrary Torah indicates clearly that pig should not be taken for it doesn't cud, though has cloven hoof"

But you just now said that Old Testament is the part of Bible... It means Bible also does not permit eating pig. How's that people of faith as per Bible eat ham?"

"I don't know!" He just shrugged his shoulder. He was getting nervous guessing my next move.

"But Qur'ãn, I am told, prohibits ham in clear proclamation..."

"May be!" My Jew companion who was so excited with his knowledge of religions about Judaism, Christianity and Islam, and their historical backgrounds was getting nervous. But my purpose was not to criticize or win the points. My purpose was divine, to get him the insight about the commonalties between the two religions – Judaism and Islam. I was sure, the fountainhead of these two religions is one and the same – Prophet Abraham.

My enquiring eyes were piercing him. He paused and then eventually surrendered.

"Yes, I see a lot of likeness in faith and practices between these two religions..."

"Then, why this grave misunderstanding and conflict between Jews and Muslims?" I asked pointblank.

"Bloody Ego..." He laughed. "Yes, it is sheer bloody 'Ego' that created a gulf between Jews and

Moslems." He then acquired seriousness on his face and shared his heart, taking me a Hindu.

"You see, both Jews and Arabs suffer in awful ego that does not allow to understand the common grounds. Each of us tries to prove other wrong. I agree, basically both of us believe in Prophet Abraham. But both of us suffer with egotism. We, the two nations, are very egoistic. Believe me, it is just Ego that separates us." There was a silence. The silence of sphinx!

'Ego' I started thinking. What a negative psychological status! Does any religion permit its followers to suffer from ego? I know, Qur'ãn doesn't permit ego and indicates clearly that a man of ego will not get entry in Paradise. Ego is nothing but the reflection of one's inadequacy within. Islam is a very profound religion. Those who truly believe in Islam and follow Qur'ãn can never suffer from inadequacy. If such inadequacy, what is called Ego, really persists, someone needs to raise his voice and say, 'Hello, Mr. Ego stop it. Ego and Islam do not go together.'

I am not coming to a conclusion agreeing with Mr. Jew. But, simultaneously I would not like to brush aside the view. It is better if each of us, self-instrospectively, clean the heart and mind and say with confidence, "No, I don't suffer from ego. I am a true Muslim." Any 'inadequacy' is not akin to Islam.

Islam...

It was a pleasant breezy mcrning on the open

terrace of Hotel Fairmont in San Francisco. Every morning used to start with meditation as followed in different religions. The conductor told the participants in clear terms that the purpose of meditation was to discover the universe within and get connected to cosmic whole.

It was Deepak Chopra – a medical doctor by practice, a scientist by learning, and a spiritual master by recognition – who conducted the meditation that morning. After the meditation while he was explaining 'spirituality' I noted two points strongly. 'Spirituality is understanding the Whole'. Then he concluded saying, 'Surrendering to God is the pre-requisite of spirituality. When you surrender, surrender to Him unconditionally."

After the meditation we gathered on the open terrace where the morning tea was served. I caught Deepak when the crowd around him thinned down.

"Deepak," I called him with his first name, as everyone used to call in the US and shared with him something that he really admired. I shared with him that the true meaning of Islam is 'unconditional surrender to Allah'. A man of knowledge and master of a broad mind as Deepak was, appreciated this input. I could read this from his face. A very humble person, down to earth, not inflated with the popularity and recognition he has earned across the globe. In the US he is considered as a rare genius who can teach science to the scientists. I requested him to let his participants know through him the real meaning of

Islam – the meaning that Deepak attached to true spirituality.

Then I asked a very funny question and he almost looked at me with the eyes saying, 'what a stupid question!' I asked, "Deepak when it comes to 'monotheism' why only three religions are quoted in books and encyclopedia – Judaism, Christianity, and Islam?"

"Because they are the only monotheistic religions..."

"What about Hinduism?" I asked

"No, it is not a monotheistic religion – we believe in plurality of god."

"When you say, 'we' you mean Hindus or 'Hinduism'?" I asked. He kept quiet. I waited for a while and then proceeded. "Deepak, I have read Vedas – I found monotheism in its core, what in Islam is called 'Wahdaniat' (or Touheed)'. Then I recited – 'Ekko Brahammam, Duttia Nahisty', meaning there is only one God, besides Him there is no other God. He preferred to maintain silence. But he was listening to me with his full concentration. Then I came to Hindu Trinity and said, "the three attributes of God – the creator, the sustainer, the destructor – are but the traits which have been conditioned and personified for the purpose of understanding..." He was listening to me carefully, while taking the sip of hot coffee. Then, I shared with him that as per Qur'ãn there are 99 attributes of God, which a common Muslim calls as

Allah's names. Someone may mistake these 'attributes' as 'personalities', and create multiple gods, which an authentic Muslim will not do for his faith and belief in singularity of God is firm. Then, I explained my understanding.

"What I understand, there is no basic difference in Hinduism in accepting one God as the almighty; the difference is only in understanding differently His attributes." Then, I shared with him the explanation given by Swami Chinmayananada in the introductory chapter to 'Kenopanisad', where he mentioned clearly that 'Absolute Truth' couldn't be explained in words, or through images or idols. "He explained the Vedic meaning of Supreme Reality. He calls Him the total causal body of the universe. He also speaks of Supreme God. It is connotation of language and understanding of attributes..." I looked at him. He was listening to me carefully.

"In that sense, yes... What you say makes sense," was his simple and brief reply. I was excited. He outright didn't reject my views and my understanding of Vedas as monotheistic scripture.

I conclude my understanding of Islam – a religion of universality and humanism with a quotation from Holy Qur'an:

O mankind! We created you from a single (pair) of a male and a female, and made you into nations and tribes, that ye may know each other (not that ye may despise each other).

May God give us the wisdom to understand the unity in diversity. May God give us the will to bring the nations and races nearer to each other and not to despise each other. May God give us the intellect to understand the meaning of 'non-judgmental justice in spirituality. May God correct me, if I have erred in understanding the true meaning of Islam.

It is 'intention', not the meaning attached to it, that matters.

Purity of intent is the purity of faith – words that explain and become the cause of interpretation are secondary.

My intent is pure.

*****

KUN...

Today we live in the spacetime, discovered by Albert Einstein.

Yesterday we lived in Newton's lonely space.

Tomorrow, we will perhaps live in Stephan Hawking's baby universes.

Yesteryears...

About two thousand years ago, we lived in the ill-discovered cosmos of Ptolemy – a great Greco-Egyptian mathematician and astronomer of second century AD – with the Earth in the centre of the universe. The Ptolemaic belief was challenged just four hundred years back.

Two thousand and six years ago, we lived in Aristotle's perceived universe through astronomical favours, with fewer heavenly bodies around us.

And six millenniums ago we lived in the world rested on the back of a big tortoise!

Amazing!

Is the cosmos changing every year, every century, or every millennium? Obviously not! Science believes that cosmos had come into existence ten to twenty billion years ago. The cosmos has certainly gone through cosmological changes, but it didn't emerge on the back of a big tortoise. Nor did our universe pass through the 'phases of ignorance' at particular cuts of time, as and when great mathematicians, astronomers and scientists made the discoveries. What changed from time to time is our knowledge about cosmos.

How perfect is our knowledge of mathematics, astronomy and science? The answer is obvious; it is perfectly imperfect. The journey is on and the enigma of universe remains as a perfect story of mystery. At every cut of time, as and when a new discovery was made we discovered a new cosmos. I don't know should I call it funny or stupid. How feeble is the knowledge of science yet we boast!

Until a few centuries ago we followed what we had learnt from Aristotle in the fourth century BC. We held the Ptolemian belief of second century AD for many centuries, believing that the Earth was the centre of the universe. Until recently, we knew only five planets. Today we discovered 9 heavenly bodies in our Solar Systerm; the discovery of Pluto is quite latest in terms of cosmic time.

How perfect is our Knowledge or knowledges? Do we need words to explain?

Human Knowledge! It's so imperfect...

What we know is nothing! What we do not know is almost everything.

If the human knowledge were perfect, Socrates,

the genius, wouldn't have said, I know, I know 'nothing'. I am ignorant of absolute truth. But I am humble before my ignorance and therein lies my honor and my reward.

If we just understand our ignorance, this awareness will create a Smart Bang of new understanding, bigger than the Big Bang.

The sage of Lebanon, Kahlil Gibran discovers a new truth. He considers the vacancy that remains as ignorance in the mind as a blessing. He says: "Had I filled myself with all that you know, what room should I have for all that you do not know?" Think! The meaning is much deeper than appears at surface.

Likewise, had we frozen our entire mind-space with Aristotelian knowledge about cosmos, what room did we find for all that which we discovered later, through the knowledge of Newton, Einstein, Carl Sagan, Stephen Hawking... Yesterday's knowledge is Today's ignorance. And if the quest goes on to uncloak the mystery-story, today's knowledge will be tomorrows' ignorance. I thank the almighty for my ignorance – He didn't fill the entire mind-space with imperfect knowledges. This vacancy in my mind, caused by the divine hand, is keeping my urge alive for learning and becoming aware of subtle things.

The ignorant people make tall claims about their knowing; those who know are so humble confessing their ignorance.

The scientists were equally humble when it comes

to knowing the Cosmos fully. Modesty is akin to greatness. Ptolemy and Kepler were disarmingly modest. So was Sir Isaac Newton: "I do not know what I may appear to the world; but to myself I seem to have been like a boy playing on the seashore, and diverting myself, in now and then finding a smoother pebble or prettier shell than ordinary, while the great ocean of truth lay all undiscovered before me."

Everyone is ignorant when it comes to new discovery.

Knowledge shapes the philosophical view. Knowledge can be original, the acquired one, or wisdom based. Knowledge can be procured one through logical conclusion, inspirational, intuitive or some sort of inspired guess. Knowledge can also be acquired through some idealized experiments. There are many ways to discover truth.

The knowledge acquired by mankind in the BC era was through sages, saints, spiritual teachers, Zen masters, Sufis, and philosophers. Such knowledge was mostly spiritual, intuitive and, in certain cases, rather inspired guess. Yes, great masters like Confucius, Socrates, Plato, Aristotle, Pythagoras, Chanakya etc., gave logical buttress to their thoughts and philosophy. For sure their knowledge was not scientific; it was not of lesser value or of lower rank, nevertheless.

We are so excited with the yet-to-be-perfect

knowledge of science and astronomy that we shy away our religious beliefs. To express our 'modernity' we behave ourselves royal than the king.

The king of astronomy who passed away a few years back – Carl Sagan – gives a unique place to the religious beliefs vis-à-vis science. "The chief difference between them – religious myths and modern scientific myth of the big bang – is that science is self-questioning, and that we can perform experiments and observation to test our ideas. But those other creation stories (in various religions) are worthy of deep respect."

When Albert Einstein calls the creation process as a mystery story or Carl Sagan a creation story, neither mean story in the conventional sense of fiction. The great scientists feel so humble before religion and take the Holy Scriptures worthy of respect.

'Kun' is the key word in Islamic belief. The Cosmos was caused with the command of Allah – 'Kun' meaning 'be it'! The description in Torah, Old Testament or Bible is no much different. The Holy Scriptures describe the creation with the command of God, who said, 'Let there be...'

The creation of cosmos is a perfect mystery. The Creation Hymn in Rig-Veda also calls it a mystery story. "... Who really knows? Who will here proclaim? Whence was it (Cosmos) produced?" The creation story is filled with mystery!

In good olden days the sages tried to discover the cosmos through their intuitive eye.

Modern experiments show that the human mind can operate from another plane, the faculty of intuition. Most of us, at some time or the other, have experienced that gut feeling invariably comes true. There is no rational explanation as to why you feel what you do but there it Is, and there ends the matter.

To understand Cosmology and to grasp the in-depth insight of Holy Scriptures, one needs to think and understand from a higher 'plane'. A cursory approach at one end, and 'splitting hair' at the other, will not take us to the higher plane where 'intuitive connectivity' becomes effortless. It appears both, Isaac Newton and Albert Einstein worked on 'Cosmology' from an intuitive plane and discovered much more than what they gave to us. They were afraid of disclosing the subtle truth discovered by them through their intuitive wisdom. As a Scientist none of them could share with the world, as the discovered truth could not be proved scientifically. They never wanted to lose their image as a 'Scientist'. What they have given to us as scientists is a very small share of their massive discoveries.

Intuition is when we know, but we don't know how we know, explains Nancy Rosanoff in 'Intuition Workout'. Today, ESP (Extrasensory Perception) is a science, which lets you know the truth, without insisting or questioning, 'How you know it'.

Intuitive thinking!

Sometimes we need to see through the third eye. Sometimes we need to react through what is called sixth sense. Most of the cosmic discoveries in the BC era were made through intuitive thinking. "How do I know the ways of all things at the beginning? By what is within me" the old master, Lao Tzu, said once.

Science cannot be taken the be-all and the end-all. It suffers from its own limitations. The limitations are not unknown, they are known and agreed one – old physics, traditional physics, quantum physics, modern physics, classical physics... What was modern yesterday has become traditional today.

I heard scientists saying in the global convention held by State of the World Forum in San Francisco in October 1999, "Not being proved scientifically no way undervalues the quality and genuineness of the knowledge. The time has come the scientists should say a bit forcefully that we need not prove through mathematical equations what we have discovered." Intuition is a superior knowledge; it is beyond laboratory tests and scientific conclusions, though.

In the journey of six milleniums through spacetime what we could gather so far is: The only world on which we know with certainty that the matter of the Cosmos has become alive and aware. The journey that began with 'Earth as the flat plate supported on the back of a big tortoise' is just half way today, even after discovering Newton's lonely space, and Einstein's vibrating and living spacetime. What we boast about our knowledge of billions and billions of galaxies expanding in the infinite Cosmos, will remain infinitesimally insignificant and puny after a century or a millenium, I suppose. There are no dead-ends in the discovery of cosmos. The journey of discovery of Cosmos through science is infinitely long.

In my imagination, there exists the perfect mystery story – a story, which may perhaps be true to the man's conquest of his own ignorance.

However, Stephen Hawking does not seem to agreeing that creation of Cosmos is a 'Mystery story'. "I don't agree with the view that the universe is a mystery, something that one can have intuition about but never fully analyze or comprehend." However, in the same breath the genius admits the fact: "There is still a great deal that we don't know or understand about the universe." Eventually, Hawking also seems to be a companion of Newton's boy playing on the seashore of Timelessness. However, he is quite optimistic and strongly feels that a complete understanding of universe may not be beyond our power. The clock of time can alone show us, What awaits in the spacetime!

While I touch upon Torah, Zabur, Bible, and Qur'ãn vis-à-vis exploration of Cosmology, I find some Vedic content relating to the context: Creation Hymn – 10.129, Rig-Veda.

'There was neither 'non-existence' nor 'existence'

then; there was neither the realm of space nor the sky which is beyond. What stirred? Where? In whose protection? Was there water, bottomlessly deep? There was neither death nor immortality then. There was no distinguishing sign of night nor of day. That one breathed, windless, by its own impulse. Other than that, there was nothing beyond.'

'Darkness was hidden by darkness in the beginning; with no distinguishing sign, all this was water. The life force that was covered with emptiness, that one arose through the power of heat.'

'Who really knows? Who will here to proclaim it? Whence was it produced? Whence is this Creation? The 'Devas' came afterwards, with the creation of this universe. Who then know whence it (cosmos) has arisen?'

The Ultimate Truth, the creator — call Him with any name – was in existence prior to the 'Devas' came into being, proclaims Rig Veda. In Hinduism, Nirankari bhakti holds a highest place, most difficult to understand and practice, for its basis is to worship the formless.

Allah is formless and beyond comparison:

"Allah, is the One; Allah, who depends on none and all others depend on Him, He begets not; nor was He begotten. And there is none comparable to Him."

(Ikhlas— 112:1-4)

I invite your attention. I want you to read with a

deeper understanding. I am going to touch a very subtle point, which needs an intelligent insight.

On the one hand, the ultimate truth is so pure that the human intellect feels helpless to grasp it. On the other, the restless urge in human nature is to have a vision of this ultimate truth is genuine enough and quite understandable. In some of the non-monotheistic religions, perhaps, this urge forced followers to 'condition' the ultimate truth giving the form to the formless. "The Aryan philosophy," believes Maulana Azad, "in its urge to behold the ultimate truth 'in vision', personified God Himself, thereby throwing the doors open in image worship – symbolic representation of the gods and goddesses."

There're two ways to understand the supreme truth. One is by qualifying the Absolute with attributes; the other is by depriving Him of all attributes. "It was the other process what was particularly followed by the Upanishads – the process of negations, 'Neti, Neti'," writes Maulana Azad. The process of negation, or call it 'Neti, Neti' was the style of explanation in the sixth century BC, though there was no common link between two thinkers thinking the same way, then. For instance, Socrates' teachings were through the process of negation. 'What is justice?' 'What is virtue?' Such intangible values he explained through the process of elimination of wrong answers. One may call it the process of 'Neti, Neti'.

Faith is much deeper than thoughts for it lives intuitive values; Faith begets faith. 'Intention' is the soul of thoughts and actions. My intentions are pure – universality of humankind and to contribute my bit in bringing about peace on this planet of life where life is shattering between the distances created by men.

Now a few steps towards bridging the islands of isolation... Returning to creation hymn of Rig-Veda:

"Darkness was hidden by darkness in the beginning; with no distinguishing sign, all this was water..."

"There was neither 'non-existence' nor 'existence' then; there was neither the realm of space nor the sky which is beyond. What stirred? Where? In whose protection? Was there water, bottomlessly deep?"

Was there water bottomlessly deep? Was in the beginning all that was water? These are the questions, which ring many bells in the mind while reading the creation hymn in Rig-Veda.

Now I quote Qur'ãnic verse – Surah Hud – 7:

"He is Who created the heavens and the Earth in six days – and His Throne was over the Waters..."

The religions that appear to be so different; amidst the diversity there lies a unique unity underneath...

Returning to 'non-existence' in Vedic text...

'Existence' came from 'Non-existence'. There was neither 'Non-existence' nor 'Existence' then.

Think!

Think between the distances of your quiet

moments. Listen, what I say under my breath. Sensitize the probability waves to resolve the truth of wholeness.

Darkness was hidden by darkness in the beginning. Like a peel of onion, existence came from non-existence. However, there was something anterior to non-existence. Mind goes not. Our sensory perception is not sensitive enough to comprehend the beginning of cosmos, which came into existence from non-existence, while something beyond non-existence was still in being. What was waiting prior to non-existence? The mystery of creation of cosmos seems to unanswerable. But That's unanswerable', is no answer.

Was it the Supreme Truth that existed prior to non-existence? The continuum! The unborn! The formless! The infinite! The unmanifest! The answer is 'Yes'. The Creator – call him with any name – was in existence even prior to 'non-existence'.

The Old Master, Lao Tzu, in the sixth Century BC got to the bottom of creation – the beginning of the universe is the mother of all things. He proceeded with divine reliance, as if the archangel brought the revelations unto him!

> "Something mysteriously formed,
>
> existed before heaven and earth.
>
> In the silence and the void,
>
> Standing alone and unchanging,
>
> Ever present and in motion.

Perhaps it is the mother of ten thousand things.

I do not know His name.

Call him 'Tao'.

For lack of a better word, I call Him great."

The Old Master uprightly owns up a sage's unawareness: "Some things are not favoured by Heaven. Who knows why? Even the Sage is unsure of this!" Creation of Cosmos is the perfect mystery-story... Both science and language are not capable of explaining this occurrence. The theory of Big Bang is not free from controversies, nor are free from debate the general theory of relativity and quantum mechanics.

Stephen Hawking in his 'Black Holes and Baby Universes' makes it clear: "The general relativity brings about its own downfall by predicting singularities. In order to discuss the beginning of universe, we need a theory that combines relativity with quantum mechanics." The gap needs to be filled, to explain the origin of Cosmos through scientific favors. A unified scientific theory, Hawking, at present, is working upon.

To understand the cosmic mystery the scientists of new century are working on what they call 'bootstrap' technique – a single theory that should be able to bind all the theories which stand scattered in bits and pieces.

Before we understand cosmology through Qur'ãnic verses, let us see how other primitive thoughts explain the creation theory.

Heraclitus, a Greek philosopher born in the 6th century BC, believed in a unique cosmic principle that there is no permanent reality except the reality of 'change', a position illustrated by his famous maxim: You cannot step twice in the same river. Thus, the only possible real state is the transitional one of Becoming – the Present.

Another Greek philosopher, Pythagoras (582-507 BC) is known for his mystical brotherhood is also the gratuity of the middle of sixth century BC. We know little of his life and nothing of his writings; all of our knowledge comes from his followers, the Pythagoreans. The Pythagoreans were also among the first to discover and teach that the earth is a spherical planet. But they believed that it revolves about a fixed point. Beginning with the discovery of numerical relations between musical notes, they taught that the essence of the truth of wholeness was number. They believed that all relationships and the cosmic patterns – even abstract ones – could be expressed numerically.

'Chaos' in Greek mythology means Space and 'Gaea', the Earth. Gaea (Earth) is considered daughter of 'Chaos' (space). The Greek mythology describes the cosmic existence in terms of 'Chaos theory':

'Chaos' in Greek mythology means the vacant, unfathomable space from which everything arose. In the Olympian myth 'Gaea' sprang from Chaos and became the mother of all things.

As per Greek mythology, this way, the invisible, unfathomable cosmos arose in the vacant space. Earth sprang from space and became the mother of all things.

Buddhism, for many centuries, dominated spiritual traditions in most parts of Asia, including of Indochina, as well as Sri Lanka, Nepal, Tibet, China, Singapore, Korea and Japan. Buddha was not curious about the origin of cosmos or nature of divinity – his concern was human situations such as suffering and frustration of human beings.

Buddha's last words while he was breathing his last, characterize his cosmic view on inescapable decline: Decay is inherent in all compound things; strive on with diligence. It was perhaps Buddha, who discovered first, the second law of thermodynamics – entropy. Again, it was Buddha who was the first Fuzzy-logist as per Lotfi Zadeh, who developed Fuzzy logic.

Coming back to ancient China, in sharp resemblance to the Greek duet – Chaos and Gaea – is Chinese mythos. Tai-Chi-T'u or the diagram of Supreme Ultimate describes the cosmic truth by counterbalancing Yin and Yang. "Cosmic principle", says Chuang Tzu, a staunch follower of Lao Tzu, "are blended harmony of the Yin and Yang."

"In its original cosmic sense, the Tao is the ultimate, undefinable reality and as such it is the equivalent of the Hinduist Brahman and Buddhist Dharmakaya," observes Fritjof Capra, a modern physicist and the author of 'The Tao of Physics'. In my view, Lao Tzu's Tao was formless. 'Tao' can be translated as 'Path' or 'Straight Path'. But in its truest sense, Lao Tzu's intent of Toa was the essence of the universe. Tao can also be understood as the cosmic process – manifestation. Tao is very much in similitude to Vedic Absolute Truth – formless.

"Absolute Truth cannot be explained in words... Any amount of intellectual understanding of the Conditioned Brahman will not take us to our goal." Swami Chinmayananda in the introductory chapter to 'Kenopanisad' makes a very revealing assertion clarifying the Vedic meaning of Supreme Reality, what he calls as God-principle, the 'total causal body' of the universe:

"The sum total of all the intellect of all the 'Jiva-s' that are living in the visible world, the 'jagat', is the conception of God. Not our conception of a God, as Rama, Krisna, Siva, Christ or Muhammad, but the Total Concept, the God-Principle. The particular incarnation (Avatar-s) are only manifestations of, the God-Principle. God is the Total Causal Body of the Universe."

With my apologies to revered Swami

Chinmayananda, who seems to be unacquainted with the basic Islamic faith, I wish to make clear that 'Muhammad' is never considered God by Muslims, nor does Islam permit such blasphemy.

Let me halt here and clarify some basic misconceptions about Islam first.

Islam is not Mohammedism as made to believe by the Western world with manipulative intentions – one must understand this clearly. Islam exists from the day one; Adam was the first prophet of Muslims. This may shake and shock those who know not the basics of Islam; I am not excluding some of Muslims who are unenlightened, they regularly pray five times, though!

Muhammad is the name of holy prophet and the Qur'ãnic verses were revealed unto him. On the analogy of Taoism, Buddhism, Zoroastrianism, Confucianism and the like, the Western writers called Islam as Mohammedism and Muslims as Mohammedans.

Without knowing even the basics of Islam people try to cut up Islam...

Most of the non-Muslims take Muhammad to Muslims in the sense as Christ is God to Christians or Krishna is a re-carnation of Vishnu to Hindus. Those who make references from Islam without understanding the basics must know that Prophet Mohammed was a human being; he was but a man. Qur'ãn asks Prophet Muhammad to proclaim:

'Say (O Mohammed): Glory to my Lord,

I am but a man,

Who has come to you

As His Messenger.

I am nothing more.' (Al-Isra—17:93)

Qur'ãn again and again asks Prophet Muhammad to reveal unto the mankind:

'Say: I have no power to do any good or bad, even to myself,

Only God has the power and does as He pleases.

If I had the knowledge about the unseen

I would have enjoyed abundance of good,

And no evil would have befallen me.

Verily, I am just a Warner

And a bringer of glad tidings

To those who believe in God.' (Al-Araf—7:188)

Prophet Muhammad was a human being. The famous parable that brings monotheism in sharp focus in the context, is an irrefutable reference, I believe.

Not many hours had passed since the Prophet's death, when Abu Bakr, the first Caliph of Islam, ascending the pulpit proclaimed: He who worshipped Muhammad, let him know that Muhammad is dead; and he who worshipped Allah, let him know that Allah lives always. He never dies.

"It was done simply to prevent the prophet from ever being hailed as God or as His incarnation, or invested with the 'attributes' and honour exclusive to God," is the inference drawn by Maulana Abul Kalam Azad. I have read his 'Tafseer' of Qur'ãn in Urdu. Like Iqbal, he was also misunderstood by most of Muslims probably for the reason that both of them scale height and talk from the plane not in reach of the knowledge of a common man. Maulana's language was Arabic. He had the mastery over Arabic language. He was a great linguist. He not only knew the meaning, but also knew what meaning was given to a particular word at particular cut of time. He was one of such Muslim scholars who understood the meaning of Islam and Qur'ãn in a holistic perspective.

Islam dared to explain the absolute truth without any 'conditioning'. One must understand the limitations of our intellect. To overcome, we must use our intuitive wisdom to go beyond where the intellect can take us – conditioning of the ultimate truth will mislead. We may mistake the 'conditioned object' as the ultimate truth. It happened to many, many a time. For instance, there is no scope of 'image worship' in the teachings of Buddha. His last message was, "See that you do not worship my ashes. If you do, the path of salvation will be closed to you." In fact, Buddha's faith in monotheism was so powerful that he did not dare to capture God even in 'mental image' for God is so subtle and 'image-less'. "Likewise, the teaching of Christianity originally concentrated on 'unity of God'," writes Maulana. "But within one hundred years of his advent, Christ himself was raised to the position of God by his followers."

Now, let us understand narration on creation of the world advanced by Holy Torah – Christian name for Hebrew Scriptures is Old Testament that forms the first portion of the Christian Bible. I begin with the text from the Revised Standard Version of the Bible:

"In the beginning God created the heavens and the Earth.

The earth was without form, and void; darkness was on the face of the deep. And Spirit of God was hovering over the face of the waters."

Jews and Christians may not perhaps be aware of the likeness that lies alive in the creation song of Rig Veda: 'Darkness was hidden by darkness in the beginning; with no distinguishing sign, all this was water...'

The purpose of my lifework is not to pickup the holes, but to fill the void with relevance that catches the scarce-eye of wisdom. People tend to insulate one's faith giving it names, slicing it off from the cosmic truth. The Truth of Wholeness exists in togetherness – the dissimilarities could be simply and safely assigned to the human factor. Some noticeable 'variances' would be the result of 'human factor' and sometimes the reflection of human understanding.

The ultimate truth can never be dissimilar to different sects of humankind. The variation lies in one's understanding, interpretation, misquotation, corruption or dilution of facts, manipulation, or misjudgment. Reasons can be many, but each relates to 'human factor'.

To proceed with the text of Old Testament, as available today:

"Then God said, 'Let there be light', and there was light. And God saw that the light was good; and God separated the light from the darkness. God called the light 'day', and the darkness he called 'night'. And there was evening and there was morning, one day.

And God said, 'Let there be a firmament in the midst of the water, and let it separate the waters from the waters'. And God made the firmament and separated the waters, which were under the firmament from the waters, which were above the firmament. And God called the firmament Heaven. And there was evening and there was morning, a second day.

And God said, 'Let the waters under the heaven be gathered together into one place, and let the dry land appear.' And it was so. God called the dry land Earth, and the waters that were gathered he called Seas... And God saw that it was good. And there was evening and there was morning, a third day.

And God said, 'Let there be lights in the firmaments of the heavens to separate the day from night; and let them be for signs and for seasons and for days and years, and let them be lights in the firmament of the heavens to give light upon the earth.' And it was so... And God saw that it was good. And there was evening and there was morning, a fourth day.

And God said, 'Let the waters bring forth swarms of living creatures, and let birds fly above the earth across the firmament of the heavens.' So God created the great sea monsters and every living creature that moves, with which the waters swarm, according to their kinds, and every winged bird according to its kind. And God saw that it was good... And there was evening and there was morning, a fifth day.

And God said, 'Let the earth bring forth living creatures according to their kinds: cattle and creeping things and beasts of the earth according to their kinds.' And it was so. And God made the beasts of the earth according to their kinds and the cattle according to their kinds, and everything that creeps upon the ground according to its kind. And God saw that it was good.

Then God said, 'Let us make man in our image, after our likeness; and let them have dominion over the fish of the sea, and over the birds of the air, and over the cattle, and over all the earth and over every creeping thing that creeps upon the earth.' So God created man in his own image, in the image of God he created him; male and female he created them... And God saw everything that he had made, and behold, it was very good. And there was evening and there was morning, a sixth day.

Thus the heavens and earth were finished, and all the host of them. And on the seventh day God finished his work which he had done, and he rested on the seventh day from all his work which he had done. So God blessed the seventh day and hallowed it, because on it God rested from all his work which he had done in Creation."

The biblical assent on 'creation of the cosmos' in six days, where the 'day' was described in terms of 'there was evening and there was morning', warrants elaboration and some meaningful deliberations – I shall deal this later.

This is the biblical version of genesis, 'How the heavens and earth were created'! In the description of the seventh day, the expression 'He (God) rested', is a manner of translating the Hebrew word 'Sabbath', from which the Jewish day for rest is derived – 'Sabbath'. It is believed that the Jews followed

'Saturday' as Sabbath, which shifted to 'Sunday' by the Christians.

The text from Torah is quoted above, as it is available today in the biblical version genesis.

Six hundred years after Christ, the Qur'ãnic verses were revealed unto Prophet Muhammad as the divine manifestation via the archangel – Gabriel.

'Apparently', Creation story in Qur'ãn is very similar to the one in the Bible or Torah:

"Your guardian-lord is God Who created the heavens and the earth in six days... " (Al-Araf—7:54).

But an in-depth study of Qur'ãnic Cosmology makes an audible difference. The difference could be due to differing in understanding of truthful words of God with the passage of time, due to human factor.

Qur'ãn does not provide a unified description of the Creation. Instead of a continuous narration, there are passages dispersed all over the holy book which deal with certain aspects of the Creation and provide information on the successive events making its development in correspondence with the text of relevance.

Again, back to six days, the day is not the same as perceived by Biblical reading. "There is absolutely no ambiguity whatsoever in the Biblical description of the Creation in six days followed by a day of rest, the Sabbath. The way the Bible interprets the interval of time between two successive sunrises or sunsets for inhabitant of Earth," writes the author of 'The Bible, The Qur'ãn and Science', Maurice Bucaille. "The Creation for the Islamic Revelation also took place over a period of six days. But the word used in Qur'ãn for a day is Yom, plural, ayyam in Arabic – the plural ayyam can mean, not just 'day', but also long length of time – an indefinite period of time (but always long)." This way, more appropriately, six days can also be interpreted as 'six periods' of time. This becomes absolutely clear from Surah 32, verse 5, where of Yom (day) – the period of time – is described as a measure of 'thousand year,' and in Surah 70, verse 4, Yom as a measure of '50,000 years' of our reckoning on earth.

The Qur'ãn verses make clear unto us that Time is not absolute; it is relative. What was revealed in Qur'ãn in the 6th century AD, discovered by Einstein in the 20th century. The Quranic measure of time does correspond with Albert Einstein's theory of Relativity – what appears to be a small period on Earth could be an eon on another planet in the sister galaxy. The 'time-interval' is not the same on all the planets – it varies significantly. The 'time-interval' is different on different heavenly bodies. The curvature in space causes all the difference. The eloquent proof of the fact is that the reality described by Relativity Theory cannot easily be grasped by our ordinary understanding. Each of the verses of Qur'ãn that deals with the stages in Creation in terms of Yom, meaning 'day', intends in reality 'very long periods', or ages, or aeons, is my understanding.

To quote Qur'ãn:

"He rules (all) affairs from the Heavens to the Earth; in the end will (all affairs) go up to Him, on a Day, the space whereof will be (as) a thousand years of reckoning." (As-Sajdah—32:5)

"And they will bid thee to hasten the chastisement. But God cannot fail His warning. And verily, a day with thy Lord is as a thousand years, as ye reckon them! ..." (Al-Hajj—22:46-47)

"The angels and the spirits ascend unto Him in a Day the measure whereof (as) fifty thousand years." (Al-Maarij—70: 4)

The way the Bible interprets the 'day' means the interval of time between two successive sunrises or sunsets. Qur'ãn describes the Creation in terms of ayyam – six periods with no appropriation to sunrise and sundown.

As regards God resting on Sabbath, the Qur'ãnic pledge is otherwise:

"We created the Heavens and the Earth and all between them in six days, nor did any sense of weariness touched Us." (Qaf—50:38)

God did not take any rest after creating the cosmos in six periods, or call it ayyam. A 'day' is a period or aeon as long as God wills. The Qur'ãnic version of Creation is near to science. The supreme truth – Allah, as described in Qur'ãn – does not suffer with human fatigue, that needs rest. The 99 attributes of

Allah should be understood with an intuitive mind and not in physical terms. Nor these attributes should be taken merely as names. They are profound and reflect the wholesomeness of the divinity of Lord. Let the glory of Qur'ãn be received by elating our flight of thoughts and scaling the higher altitude. Infinite cannot be grasped with finite tools. Science is a finite tool, even Hawking will agree, though he dislikes philosophers who intuit rather than withstand the scientific tests.

Before I proceed further, it is appropriate to be precise on the main points on which Qur'ãn gives us information about the Creation:

- Existence of six periods (Ayyam) for the Creation.
- Plurality of the Heavens.
- Existence of an intermediary creation 'between the Heavens and the Earth'.
- Usage of 'seven', such as 'seven Heavens' etc., can also be taken as an expression of plurality – it often carries the meaning of 'many'. The Greeks and Romans also seem to have used the number 'seven' to mean an undefined idea of plurality.

The debate about whether and how the universe began has been on from time immemorial. Hawking in his 'Black Holes and Baby Universes' makes a very revealing statement: "Many early traditions, and the Jewish, Christian and Islamic religions, held that the universe was created in the fairly recent past. In the seventeenth century Bishop Usher calculated a date of 4004 BC for the creation of the universe, a figure he arrived at by adding up the ages of people in the Old Testament."

In his 'A Brief History of Time', Stephen Hawking made a similar observation, quoting St. Augustine. "St. Augustine accepted a date of about 5000 BC for the creation of the universe according to the Book of Genesis. It is interesting that this is not so far from the end of the last Ice Age, about 10,000 BC, which is when archaeologists tell us that civilization really began."

Again, the same human factor.

I shall confine to the revelations of Qur'ãn, as I understand the holy verses. The Qur'ãn is silent on historical dates, nor does it give any indication which should make believe Hawking to conclude that as per Qur'ãn the universe was created in fairly recent past. Qur'ãn does not provide any geological sequence-line, nor geological time, nor does it give any chance for 'human factor' to make misinterpretations. I wish sincerely that Hawking must make correction in his statement and not include 'Islamic religion' along with Jewish and Christian religions while holding that as per these religions the universe was created in the recent past. Unlike the Book of Genesis, Qur'ãn does not prescribe any histogram, which may enable someone to make such guess or distracted calculations.

To intellectualize, I paraphrase Maulna Abul Kalam Azad, a genius scholar whose understanding of Qur'ãn was deep: "In the language of science, one may state that man is the latest and the noblest link in the process of creative evolution. If we look back across time to the very first impulse of life in creation, life on earth will be found to be in an immeasurably lengthy process of evolution aiming at, and culminating in the completion of man. In other words, Nature has taken billions and billions of years in its endeavor to give shape to its noblest piece of art – man."

To my mind, some readers of the Holy Scriptures mix up the revelations relating to the origin of Adam with that of beginning of cosmos. Needless to remind that Adam came into being in the Heavens and after he committed disobedience to the words of God, he was thrown from Eden Garden to the Earth. This gives clear evidence that before God created Adam, the heaven Was. The earth Was. And, thus, the cosmos Was. It is not fair to attach 'human factor' by adding our understanding to such words of God. I stand along with my firmness, and unshaken belief that the beginning of humankind with Adam, beginning of life per se, and beginning of cosmos are three different events, and Qur'ãn does not give us the liberty to club them all relating them to Adam's coming into being. If I am wrong, I wish to be corrected if someone shows me the revelations revealing otherwise. Hawking must seek apology for he is ignorant of what Qur'ãn reveals.

It is not fair to include Islam along Judaism and Christianity without having read Qur'ãn by this genius.

I first quote Surah Yunus; verse 3:

"Verily your Lord is Allah, Who created the heavens and the Earth in six Days, then He established Himself on the Throne (of Authority), regulating and governing all things..."

And verse 85, Al-Hijr states:

"We created not the heavens, the Earth, and all between, but for just ends."

Obviously, this refers to creation of the whole universe – Earth, Heavens and all between. The universe was created not but for just ends.

Verse 10 of Surah Ar-Rahman clearly indicates the purpose of creation of Earth:

'It is He (Allah) who spread out Earth for (His) creature.'

It is quite obvious from the above Qur'ãnic verse that the Earth was created for His creature – the only planet so far known for existence of life. Before life came into existence, the Earth was created. This comes out more clearly with verse 7, Surah Qaf:

"And the Earth, We have spread it out, and set thereon mountains standing firm, and produced there in every kind of beautiful growth (in pairs)."

To buttress further, I quote verse 30 from Surah Al-Baqrah:

"Behold, thy Lord said to the angels: 'I will create vicegerent on Earth'..."

Now it is very clear that Qur'ãn stands crystal clear and does not mix up the different cuts of time. To my understanding, when Allah created Adam, the Earth was already in existence. Not only Earth, but also the heavens were in existence, when God created Adam from 'sounding clay, from mud moulded into shape'. As per Islamic belief, Jin-kind was created about 2000 years before Adam was created.

Thus, the creation of the universe, the creation of the Earth, the creation of mineral kingdom, the creation of life, the creation of the animal kingdom, creation of Jin-kind and the creation of mankind are different events with different cuts of time as per my understanding of Qur'ãnic revelations. It is not fair to mix up these events occurred at different cuts of time with the human factor and draw a conclusion, which is not correct. The belief of a true Muslim can never be different from the Qur'ãnic revelations. Understanding is a human factor, though. It is the 'intent' that makes the belief perfect or shaky – words are only floats.

As mentioned above, yet, there's another creature, besides the humankind – Jinn race. The creation of Jinn race was anterior to creation of Adam. Though modern science doesn't acknowledge Jin race, some spiritual scientists do recognize this invisible race. Gary Zukav in his 'The Seat of Soul' makes a mention about such invisible souls, besides the visible human beings.

Before mankind was created, God created Jinn race from the fire of a scorching wind. "And Jinn race, We had created before, from the fire of a scorching wind." (Al-Hijr—15:27). Verse 15 of Surah Ar-Rahman reinforces this further: "And He created Jinns from fire free from smoke."

Big Bang...

Now setting the organ of sight on scientific cosmology...

The cosmos came into being ten to twenty billion years ago. However, the Earth on which we live is a 4.5 to 5 billion years old planet. Moreover, it is believed that human evolution had begun about 5 million years ago, and the human civilization can be traced to around 10,000 years of rootlets – the Ice Age came to an end in 10,000 years BC that marks the beginning of civilization.

The geological time, or call it earth's history, as per the concise Columbia Encyclopedia, is divided into five periods:

1. **Azoic time** (4,550 – 3800 million years ago)
2. **Precambrian time** (3800 – 700 million years ago)
3. **Paleozoic time** (700 – 230 million years ago). This era is subdivided into six periods.

- Cambrian period (700 – 500 million years ago)
- Ordovician period (500 – 435 million years ago)
- Silurian period (435 – 395 million years ago)

- Devonian period (395 – 345 million years ago)
- Carboniferous period (345 – 280 million years ago)
- Permian period (280 – 230 million years ago)

4. **Mesozoic time** (230 – 65 million years ago).

   This era is subdivided into three periods:

- Triassic period (230 – 195 million years ago)
- Jurassic period (195 – 140 millions ago)
- Cretaceous period (140 – 65 million years ago)

5. **Cenozoic time** (65 million – 10,000 years ago). This era is subdivided into two periods – the age of mammals:

- Tertiary period (65 million – 1.8 million years ago)
- Quaternary period (1.8 million – 10,000 years ago)

The formation of Earth took almost 750 million years – in Azoic time there was no trace of any form of life. The earliest marine life is believed to have the traces only from the fag end of the Precambrian time, 3000 millions ago. However, life in the forms of ferns, insects, cockroaches is believed to have originated in the Paleozoic time, 700 million years ago. First shark with vertebrate Jaw perhaps took form in Silurian p

eriod of Paleozoic era, 400 million years ago. Fish dominated in the Devonian period and it is guessed that the land animals also took form in the same period.

Insects like cockroaches, and first reptiles appeared towards end of Carboniferous period, 350 million years ago. In Triassic period of Mesozoic era, there were fewer species with higher population – snails were present 200 million years ago. First dinosaur and mammals may have developed in the same Triassic period, say 200 million years ago. Early birds appeared in Jurassic period, say around 150 million years ago – reptiles dominated end.

Giant apes – beginning of mankind – can be traced in Cenozoic times, almost 5 million years ago. Around 2 million years ago Stone Age began – stone-tools, fire, communal hunting, beliefs, systems, sorcery black magic and beliefs in super-naturals were the accent. The roots of human civilization can be traced to end of quaternary period, 12,000 years ago. The spiritualism and divinity also grew in the cradle of civilization, thence. Prophets came on the Earth from time to time to communicate the message of God.

NotApe but man with the backup civilization marked the distinction from animal world and human world – a journey from body to intellect. 'Animality' is the state in which the body is not associated with intellect or soul. It should be realized that the body, the mind and the soul together constitute 'human being'. And as per Torah, Zubur, Bible and Qur'ãn, this beginning began with the origin of Adam. I would not misinterpret these scriptures with human judgement, misreckoning the beginning of mankind with the beginning of cosmos or beginning of life on our planet. They are different events and Qur'ãn has not made any reference, which gives us the liberty to mix up the events. Beginning of human-life on the Earth cannot and should not be misunderstood as the beginning of cosmos with Allah's command, Kun.

We boast on our scientific knowledge. But most of us do not know that for quite many centuries Science considered a part of solar system as the universe, then for quite sometime solar system remained as universe in human imagination. Until recently Science took Milky Way as the universe or cosmos. How many of us know that only in 1924 an American astronomer, Edwin Hubble, recognized that some of the nebulae are not within our galaxy, but separate galaxies at great distances from Milky Way. Galaxies are large aggregation of gas, dust, and billions of stars. They are held together by gravitational attraction and their rotational motion prevents them from collapsing.

How puny are we; how much to no avail are our organs of perception; how much feeble are our perceptive values; how hazy is our perception – is anybody's guess who has wisdom and insight! And with such feeble human perceptions, we dare to challenge nature. Stupid!

"A semi-invisible rash of skin on a sub-microscopic planet in a second rate solar system," David Block, an Astronomer describes the infinitesimally small status of the Earth vis-à-vis the cosmos.

Again, the concept of the Supreme Reality is an undisputed reality in all the religions of the world – right from the Vedic period to the modern times. Practices may differ, though. But practices are not the true reflection of what revealed unto prophets from time to time. Every religion came with a subtle message; every time the followers made this subtle as solid, debasing for human factor.

The big bang theory states that all of the matter and energy in the cosmos was concentrated in a very small volume that exploded between 10 and 20 billion years ago, and that the resulting expansion continues today. Cosmos, large aggregation of gas, dust, and typically billions of stars, is held together by the gravitational attractions between its parts, and its rotational motion prevents it from collapsing on itself. Whether the universe's expansion will continue or eventually halt and reverse, with the Universe collapsing in the so-called 'Big Crunch' remains unanswered by Science. Most of the religions of the world refer to 'Doomsday' – the day of judgement. Does Doomsday direct to what the cosmologists call 'Big Crunch'?

The various Holy Scriptures are pregnant with oracles and suggestiveness. They do not directly and openly express or explain, but with their 'indicative meanings' they simply guide us to the very presence of Truth.

Our scientific knowledge of cosmos cannot be based on revelation of fixed truth. In the wake of scientific research and path-breaking discoveries it will always be tentative and can never rest in certainty. "Modern physics has shown us in concrete terms, that as we penetrate further into the core of the matter, our picture of nature becomes increasingly abstract and mysterious." Kunhiraman Edappetta takes a closer look at the more abstract ideas in his article, 'Of inner space, outer space'.

The known is finite; the unknown is infinite!

Hawking has been toiling with the idea of a finite universe, which does not have boundaries. He argues on the probabilities that the origin of the curved space was without 'singularities'. If the origin of cosmos were considered without 'singularity', it would mean the cosmos existed, and not that it was created. To quote him: "The problem of the origin of the universe is a bit like the old question: Which came first, the chicken or the egg? In other words, which agency created the universe, and who created that agency?"

He proceeds further holding the same logic, "Or perhaps the universe, or the agency that created it, existed forever and didn't need to be created. Until recently, scientists have tended to shy away from such questions, feeling that they belong to metaphysics or religion, rather than to science."

I wish to split his logical observation in two parts for two reasons – to make it simple and to bring about better clarity for a common person like me:

- Perhaps the universe existed forever and didn't need to be created.
- The agency that created universe existed forever and didn't need to be created.

The second part of Hawking's observation is acceptable to any Christian, Muslim, Hindu, Sikh, Jew, and Taoists – I can say based on my reading and understanding.

But, the first part is not acceptable to more than 80% of the world population – the belief that the universe is the creation of God cannot just be brushed aside. Is it not a sufficient cause to motivate the cosmologist to ponder upon the established faith of 80% of the world population on the premise, 'The universe was created; it didn't exist forever'. Big Bang also supports this premise – the universe came into existence with bang and that it didn't exist forever.

The universe has not come into being by itself; it has been created. So, it must have a Creator.

Coming to Qur'ãnic version; it substantiates that:

"On Earth are the signs of firm beliefs, and also in your own selves: Will you not then behold them?"

(Az-Zariyat—51: 20-21)

There's no blindness blinder than 'wilful-blindness'. If one doesn't want to see the signs of firm beliefs around and within, then none can get him insight. If you don't know where to go, any road can take you there. Wouldn't it be wiser to design a premise, and then work to see whether it can be proved, and to hold our beliefs steadfast; something remaining unproven does not mean the belief is untrue. Negation of war only means that there is no war, but one cannot jump to a conclusion that there's absolute peace. Likewise, negation of proof only means that the belief could not be proved, but one cannot jump to a conclusion that it is untrue.

God is unmanifest – He begets not; nor was He begotten. And there is none comparable to Him.

The cosmos came into being with the command of God – Kun! One may call it Big Bang or give any name to that occurrence. Names are of no relevance to me. What is important is that the world came into existence with the command of God – the One and Only. Likewise the word 'Kun' can be any word in other languages. So long, it refers to command of

God, and the altitude of understanding remains the same, the purpose of a common faith is served.

"It is He Who created the heavens and the Earth in true (proportion); the day He said, 'Be', behold! it is. His word is truth..." (Al-An'am—6:73)

True proportions!

Cosmic balance among heavenly bodies in true proportion is a scientific truth today. The physicists believe that the void between two electrons in atom is proportionately equivalent to the void between two galaxies. I will discuss this in detail in one of the succeeding chapters.

The cosmos came into being with the command of Allah, 'Kun'!

*****

ALLAH-U-AKBAR

'Parroting' is not 'understanding', as much as 'hearing' is not 'listening'. Unfortunately most of us only parrot rather than understand. I know many hafizs who have memorized Qur'ãn but never made an attempt to understand its bottomless depth. Yes, memorizing Qur'ãn is holy and it serves purpose. But memorizing it with deeper understanding is more rewarding not only to Hafiz but to mankind. Holy Qur'ãn insists for a meaningful reading with understanding.

Arabic is one of the richest and ancient languages. It is not easy to understand Arabic for those who have not read it as language or literature or if the language has not come to them through their mother. Then, what are the options? Either acquire mastery over the language, its dialect, grammar, colloquial usage, historical usage with contextual meaning, or look for some authentic translation. I agree, translation cannot convey what the original language can. No translation of Lao Tzu's 'Tao Te Ching' or Confucius' 'Analects' can get one the insight of their pure thoughts what the original texts depict. The issue becomes more complex and delicate when it comes to the book of God.

If one cannot understand and grasp from the original text, the next better alternative is to understand through a good translated version. This secondary option is more pragmatic for getting command over an ancient language is not that simple.

Qur'ãn clearly subscribes to reading with understanding and explaining it with understanding. The purpose is to understand and reach to the depth so that one can make perfect his actions, thoughts, faith, and intent. To quote from Surah Qaf – 45: "Fadhakkir-bil-Qur'ãn," meaning "Explain the Qur'ãn in the manner of Qur'ãn." How can one explain unless understands it in its right perspective! The strength of Qur'ãn is its simplicity. Alas! Most people mostly satisfy their literary eagerness and in this anxiety split the hair making evident their fervour. "The limitation," as Maulana Azad observes, "was very often in favour of the complex, peculiar and out of the ordinary." His searching inquiries into Qur'ãnic teachings have disclosed to him the realistic humanism that Qur'ãn stands for.

Allah-u-Akbar!

It is simple to translate but difficult to understand. Allah is great! But do we care to understand the extent of His greatness?

If I say, "Alexander was great", I must also try to

understand how great he was! If I say you are great, I must understand first what greatness I am talking about.

Picking the thread, to understand 'Allah-u-Akbar' in its truest sense, besides understanding the language, one must also have fairly good understanding of Cosmos – the vastness of His kingdom. Simply saying, 'God is great' will not let one know the immensity of His greatness. To understand the greatness of God one must understand the vastness of His Kingdom, containing universes, heavenly bodies, the energy pattern, the energy dance, the energy response, and the gravitational and repulsive forces that keeps the universe in balance by the will of God.

This urge... The urge to understand the vastness of His kingdom took me to Astronomy – the science of Cosmology. Unfortunately most people mistake Astronomy with Astrology; the latter pertains to study of stars and their affect on human beings.

Our planet, the Earth!

Earth is the fifth largest planet of Solar System and the only one known to bearing life. Its diameter in terms of speed of light is 1/8th light second – Light travels eight times across the world in one second. Earth is approximately 4.5 to 5 billion years old planet.

Solar System!

There are nine planets in the solar system, Pluto being the latest discovery.

The Milky Way!

There are around 100 billion stars in the galaxy (The Milky Way) - belong to us. Each star is a sun with its system. In other words, there are about 100 billion solar systems in Milky Way. Most amazingly the Milky Way is not a very huge galaxy; it is quite moderate in size.

The universe!

There are billions and billions of galaxies in the universe and universe is expanding! Allahu Akbar!!

The story is not yet over. The second universe is already discovered – the biggest cosmic explosion after Big Bang has since been detected on 14th December 1997 that threw the astronomical world into a tizzy. So bright and violent was the explosion that scientists say that for about 40 seconds, it appeared to outshine all the rest of the universe. This second Big Bang is estimated to have occurred some 12 billion years ago in the young universe. Assuming the universe itself is 14 billion years old, and the Earth 4 to 6 billion years old, the second Big Bang occurred some 6 to 8 billion years before the Earth formed.

Hold your breath and listen unto my breath with full of your attention...

The knowledge about the second Big Bang is just a few years old discovery to the mankind in the cosmic time of 10 to 20 billion years of existence of cosmos. Stephen Hawking is the cosmologist of our time. He is working on black holes and peeking deep into cosmic truth. He has come to conclusion about the plurality of 'universes. In his latest book he has used the connotations, 'baby universes'. I am drawing your focus on two aspects – multiplicity of 'universes' and its scientific discovery in 1997. Holy Qur'ãn came to mankind 14 century back when the universe known to mankind was half-discovered. It was the post 'Aristotelian' universe. Hardly a few pıanets were known to mankind, which was considered as universe, then. Now you would shiver in your spine filled with divinity. Everyone has read the Surah Fatihah several times – the Qur'ãn begins with this Surah. Read again this Surah in the backdrop of the newly discovered knowledge of science:

'Praise be to Allah, the Cherisher and Sustainer (Lord) of the universes' (Al-Fatiha—1:2)

Qur'ãn proclaims Allah as Rabbil-Alameen, not Rabbil-Alam. (Alam is singular, Alameen is plural). Mankind did not kncw the plurality of universe until recently. The first scientist who talked about the plurality of universe is Stephan Hawking – a living cosmologist of our time. He is the person who claimed there are many universes; he called them as baby universes. He discovered this almost a few decades before NASA noticed the second Big Bang on 14th November 1997. But Qur'ãn proclaimed Allah as the Lord of 'Universes' in the 6th Century. Is it not sufficient divine sign to bow to Him in honour, and thank Him for bestowing upon us the Holy Qur'ãn as a great favour?

There is a repetitive reference in Qur'ãn about plurality of universes. A few translators have translated the word 'Alameen' as 'worlds', which is not appropriate to my understanding. The purpose is not to keep focus on the word, but to bring to fore the plurality of 'worlds' or 'universes'. What has become known to us through NASA on 14th December 1997 and by the scientific studies of Stephan Hawking, was revealed to humankind by Qur'ãn 14 centuries back. Amazing! Allah-u-Akbar.

Qur'ãn begins with Surah Fatihah. In the very first Surah Allah makes clear unto us that He is the Lord of the universes – Rabbil-Alameen. This message comes again and again in Qur'an. To quote from Surah As-Saffat:

"...And praise to Allah, the Lord and Cherisher of the universes." (As-saffat—37:182)

One can quote numerous Surahs from Holy Qur'an, the usage of 'Alameen', meaning universes or worlds.

The possibility of multiplicity of universes beyond two is not ruled out. Stephan Hawking's discovery of space is on. As mentioned above, the discovered, he calls 'baby universes'.

Now let us have the paradoxical understanding of greatness in terms of His creation of infinitesimally smallest space – atomic space.

Infinitesimally smallest is space that dwells in each atom. To put it in simple words, each atom consists of 99.999 percent vacant space and its subatomic particles constitute hardly .001%. Obviously, any solid particle of matter is composed of more than 99.999 percent of empty space. It is believed that the void between two electrons in atom is proportionately as empty as the space between two galaxies. The Cosmos is space! The trillions and trillions of heavenly bodies – the condensed form of field as Einstein puts it – occupy hardly .001% of the cosmic space.

One more dimension of His greatness...

The discovered truth about the dual nature of electrons in atom choked the throat of the physicists during the early 1920s. It was very difficult to understand and explain the phenomenon intellectually because 'intellectually' the forms of electrons in atom were opposite – 'matter' and 'waves' simultaneously. Their understanding suffered from what I call 'Logic's myopia'. When the physicists for the first time discovered that the ultimate particle, the electron, which is the constituent of all matter, behaves very paradoxically, they were at a loss. How to describe it? It behaves as a particle and also as a wave simultaneously. For many years there was a great controversy about how to describe the unique tendency of electrons in atom, because it does not fit in the ordinary language! They preferred to make a pointless statement rather than understanding the cosmic paradox. "Electrons,' they said "are 'particles' on Mondays and Wednesdays, and 'waves' on Tuesdays and Thursdays." The more they tried to clarify, the more they made 'paradox' sharper. But the day wisdom dawned upon them, they described that electron is both together. Since that day Physics has become Metaphysics.

Electrons exist 'whirling around' in the vacant space of atom. The velocity of their 'whirling around' is 600 miles per second. These high velocities make them appear solid, just as a fast rotating propeller appears as a solid disc. Due to this tendency, we see the condensed form of energy that we call our body. Our physical self is the finest core of dense energy. Amazing!

The heavenly bodies are in harmony because of the gravitational and repulsive forces. If the latter becomes more powerful (crosses the limit what is known as Chandrashekhar's line) the planet or star is sucked into a black hole. The key word is 'proportions' that keeps the balance and harmony.

Surah Al-Ankabut makes this reference:

'Allah created the heavens and the Earth in true proportions; Verily in that is a Sign for those who believe.' (Al-Ankabut—29:44)

The 'true proportion' that keeps the heavenly bodies in harmony without sucked into black holes was discovered hardly a couple of decades back, whereas Qur'ãn proclaimed about true proportion 14 centuries ago. Subhan Allah! (Allah is flawless)

The very fact that our knowledge even about the Earth – a grain in the vast space desert – is very little, should be sobering enough to make us humble before the greatness of God – Allah-u-Akbar, as mentioned in the Holy Qur'ãn.

He is the creator of the infinite cosmic space. He is the creator of infinitesimally small atomic space. He is the creator of trillions and trillions of stars and heavenly bodies – the infinite. He is the creator of smallest sub-atomic particles – electrons – infinitesimally small.

"For lack of appropriate word I call Him 'Great'",

said Lao Tzu 2500 years ago. Great meaning 'Akbar'...

'Allah-u-Akbar' is the message of God that is vibrating in the spacetime from the time immemorial.

*****

‘MUSIUNA’

Cosmos-a perfect mystery story!

The Cosmologists believe the cosmos has come into being due to singularity – Big Bang. This big bang is believed to have taken place 10 to 20 billion years ago. A safe assumption could be 12 billions, as believed by some of the modern astronomers.

As mentioned in the preceding chapter, the discovery of universe beyond Milky Way is not very old. Until 1924, we knew only one galaxy – Milky Way which is quite moderate in size – 100,000 light years.

Today, just in less than 100 years we have discovered that there are billions and billions galaxies in the universe. All these are ‘ink-not-dry’ discoveries in terms of cosmic time.

Einstein’s theory of Relativity is hardly a century old. He proposed this theory in the paper written in 1905. It shows that time is not a universal quantity that exists on its own, separate from Space. This theory stands to say that Future and Past are just directions, up and down, left and right, upward and downward, in what Einstein calls ‘Spacetime’.

“You can only go in the future direction in Time,

but you can go at a bit or an angle to it," says Hawking. This 'angle' or 'curvature' causes the variation in the 'unit' of Time. That is why time can pass at different rate.

Let us understand from a layman's point of view, 'How does the unit of time differ?'

Due to the law of universals gravitation each body in the universe is attracted towards another body. This pulling force makes the space curvature. Since time is the fourth dimension of pace, the spacetime is curved, not flat. Gravity is so strong that space is bent round unto itself, making it rather like the surface of the Earth.

This way, Space and Time are curved. Time cannot be same, obviously. The distance of diameter is always smaller than hemisphere.

'Geodesic' stands to show the shortest path between two points on a surface. Geodesic is made of a framework of light straight. To be more simple, the shortest path between two points will be the path of light.

Against this backdrop let us understand what Einstein has discovered for us. He looked 'gravity' with a different perspective. To him 'gravity' was not merely force like other forces; it was more a consequence of the fact that spacetime was not flat, as had been assumed in the ancient days. Gravity is 'curved' or 'warped'. Heavenly bodies, including Earth, are not made to move on a curved orbit by a force called gravity. They, therefore, follow 'geodesic' – the nearest thing to a straight path on the curved space.

The same phenomenon is applicable to light. Light rays must follow geodesics in spacetime. Space is curved means that light no longer appears to travel in straight lines in space. Like heavenly bodies, light also finds the nearest thing the straight path on the curved space.

The curvature causes all the difference in the unit of time...

Now let me borrow words from Hawking. "Time should appear to run slower near a massive body like the Earth... To someone high, it would appear that everything down below was taking longer to happen."

What Stephan has discovered now, that time moves slower near a massive body like the Earth, was made clear unto us in Qur'ãn fourteen hundred years back. Isn't a miracle! God says to mankind that a unit of time, what we call a day, is not same at the Earth and Heavens. It varies. A day at Heavens could be 1000 years of reckoning or 50,000 years of reckoning on Earth. How could this be possible? Only when time moves slow near a massive body like the Earth, as discovered by Einstein and later established as a scientific fact after several experiments.

The phenomenon that came to our knowledge hardly less than a century ago, was made clear to humankind by Qur'ãn 14 centuries ago.

"He rules (all) affairs from the Heavens to the Earth: in the end will (all affairs) go up to Him, on a Day, the space whereof will be (as) a thousand years of your reckoning." (Surah As-Sajda—32:5)

"Verily a Day in the sight of thy Lord is like a thousand years of (your) reckoning." (Al-Hajj—22:47)

"The angels and the spirits assured unto Him in a Day, the measure whereof is (as) fifty thousand years." (Surah Al-Ma'arij—70:4)

Is it not a miracle? Time is not same, was mentioned in Qur'ãn fourteen hundred years ago. It is different in reckoning – what is a day at Heavens is a thousand year of reckoning on the Earth. And the day the angels and spirits assured unto Allah in a day was of the measure of fifty thousand years of our reckoning on Earth. Sub'han Allah!

Sub'han Allah! glory be to Allah, who is flawless.

I proceed further...

It was Aristotle who first discovered in 4th century BC that Earth is round 'sphere' rather than a flat plate. In 2nd century AD, Ptolemy, a Greco Egyptian mathematician and astronomer of ancient times declared Earth as motionless at the centre of the universe with all celestial bodies revolving around it.

There were only six planets known in Kepler's time: Mercury, Venus, Earth, Mars, Jupiter and Saturn. What to talk about our knowledge of galaxy, Milky Way, billions and billions of galaxies in universe, and the cosmos per se, our knowledge about the Solar System itself was weak and limited. In 1596 Kepler, a German Astronomer and professor of mathematics wrote 'Mystrium Cosmographicum'. His discovery of cosmos with 6 planets was exciting. He called this revelation, 'Cosmic Mystery'!

Newtonian cosmos was static and lifeless. The idea of a 'static universe' and his law of gravitational force could not go well. Each star in universe is ought to be attracted towards every other star, if so how could one say 'the universe is motionless', at the constant distance from each other? Wouldn't all fall together?

The universe could not remain motionless...

On one hand the gravitational force pulls bending the spacetime as curvature. On the other hand there is also a repulsive power that becomes dominant at a critical point. If a star goes a bit farther away from each other, the repulsive forces would dominate and drive them farther apart. Purposely, I am not using the technicality of 'Chandrashekhar's critical point' for the obvious reasons – the intention is not to teach cosmology, but to understand the basic structure and processes from a layman's viewpoint.

"Newton and Einstein both missed the chance of predicting that the universe should either be contracting or expanding," observes Stephan Hawking. "One cannot really hold it against Newton, because he lived 250 years before the observational discovery of the expansion of the universe. But Einstein should have known better," Hawking makes a very observant remark. As we know, Einstein had formulated the theory of general relativity in 1915 predicting universe was expanding. Against this backdrop, it is not understandable why he remained so convinced of a 'static universe' conceived by Newton? Hawking's observation is really mind-boggling. More so, because in the nineteenth century itself evidence began to accumulate that the Earth and the rest of the universe were in fact changing with time.

"We are not yet certain how many planetary systems there are, but there seems to be a great abundance," observes Carl Sagan in his famous book 'Cosmos'. It is believed that single stars like sun should have their planetary companions. "It is still too early to be sure, but it seems that a splendid variety of planetary systems to be found through out the galaxy," writes Carl Sagan. He makes a guess: "There must be a hundred billion planetary systems in the Galaxy, awaiting exploration. Not one of those worlds will be identical to Earth. A few will be hospitable; most will appear hostile."

It was Edwin Hubble who first made the discovery of expansion of universe in 1929. The galaxies are receding from us; the cosmos is expanding. The distant galaxies are moving rapidly away from us...

"But why should the galaxies be fleeing us?" Carl Sagan raises a mind-boggling question. He makes a witty observation explaining this cosmic phenomenon. "Could there be something special about our location in universe, as if the Milky Way has performed some inadvertent but offensive act in the social life the galaxies?" After passing this observation at lighter side, he shares his considered views. "It seemed much more likely that the universe itself is expanding carrying the galaxies with it."

The existence of second universe came to our knowledge on 14th December 1997. And Stephan Hawking's study and his book 'Black Holes and Baby Universes' are as fresh as the 90s of the preceding century. Before I quote Stephan, let us remember that Qur'ãn was revealed unto the mankind 14 centuries back.

Against this backdrop I now quote Stephan Hawking from his 'Black Hole and Baby Universes':

"In real time, the universe would appear to begin its expansion at a very small radius. At first, the expansion would be what is called inflationary: that is, the universe double in size every tiny fraction of a second, just as prices double every year in certain countries."

The Cosmos is expanding!

As we have thoroughly examined above, it was Edwin Hubble who discovered just in 1929 that the distant galaxies are moving rapidly away from us; the cosmos is expending.

Qur'ãnic verses came to humankind fourteen hundred year back, when the knowledge of universe was confined to a few planetary systems.

The expansion of cosmos is the most recent and imposing discovery of modern science. Today it is firmly established that Cosmos is expanding. The only point that is left for debate is the way it is expanding.

Now let me quote a verse from Surah 'Al-Dhariyat:

"The Firmament, We have built it with power. Verily, We are expanding it."

In some translations this tendency of cosmic expansion has be mentioned as creating the 'vastness of space'. But both mean the same.

Maurice Bucaille, the author of 'The Bible, The Qur'ãn and Science' explains this audible awe:

"It was first suggested by the general theory of relativity and is backed up by physics in the examination of the galactic spectrum; the regular movement towards the red section of their spectrum may be explained by the distancing of one galaxy from another. Thus, the size of the Universe is probably constantly increasing and this increase will become bigger the further away the galaxies are from us... The following verse of the Qur'ãn (Sura 51, verse 47) where God is speaking may perhaps be compared with modern idea: 'the heaven, We have built it with power. Verily, We are expanding it.' 'Heaven' is the translation of the word 'sama' and this is exactly the extra-terrestrial world that is meant."

The author of 'The Bible, The Qur'ãn and Science' gives a vivid picture of various translations of this verse. "Hameedullah in his translation of the Qur'ãn talks of the widening of the heavens and space, but he includes a question mark," writes Maurice. His earnest urge, unquenched thirst and inquisitive enquiries at last gives him clarity and he discovers: "This is true in the case of the 'Muntakab', a book of commentaries edited by the Supreme Council for Islamic Affairs, Cairo. It refers to the expanding of the Universe in totally unambiguous terms."

The verse 47 in Surah Al Dhariyat, the word used is 'Musi'una', meaning 'to make wider' or 'more spacious', 'to extend' or 'to expand'. Some translators have translated the word as 'vastness of space'.

The discovery that the universe is expanding was

one of the great intellectual revolutions of twentieth century. It stands proved today and no explanation is needed.

Verily the cosmos is expanding by the will of God. And this was revealed unto us fourteen hundred years ago. Qur'ãn made known to us in the 6th century, what discovered yesterday by the supreme brains.

Amazing!

*****

ASH-SHAMS

The controversy...

The controversy between Roman Catholic Church and Nicolas Copernicus has become the part of astronomy. The controversy could not be put off even after Copernicus' death. What this controversy was all about! Whether the Sun moves around the Earth, which is stationary or the Earth moves around the Sun which is stationary? Which statement is correct? Today the answer is obvious. Then, it was the Sun that moved around the Earth and the Earth was stationary.

The orbiting of planets is taking place in the manner it was taking place billions of years back. Nothing has changed, except our 'knowing'. How perfect is our knowing is obvious! I will deal this separately and spin out some surprise even with my feeble knowledge of astronomy. It is not the knowledge alone but the understanding in proper perspective that gets one the cutting edge.

Today the common knowledge, not belief, is that the Earth moves around the Sun, and not the other way round. The first model – the Sun moves around the Earth, and the Earth is stationary – was the religious belief that Roman Catholic Church wanted to protect and it cost Copernicus his life and later Galileo's house arrest for committing a blasphemy of supporting Copernican theory. Every astronomer has made his observations about this controversy. Even Stephan Hawking couldn't resist.

"A simple model, however, was proposed in 1514 by a Polish priest, Nicholas Copernicus. (At first, perhaps for fear of being branded heretic by his church, Copernicus circulated his model anonymously.)" Hawking gives a vivid description of this controversy in his 'A Brief History of Time'. "Copernicus' idea was that the Sun was stationary at the center and the Earth and other planets moved in circular orbits around the Sun." This model contradicted Biblical revelations and thus Copernicus had to pay the price for creating a model against the Christian faith.

Later, Galileo and Kepler publicly supported Copernicus theory and earned the wrath of Roman Catholic Church. "Galileo, perhaps more than any other single person, was responsible for the birth of modern science," compliments Stephan Hawking. "Galileo had believed Copernican theory (that the planets orbited the Sun) since early on, but it was only when he found the evidence needed to support the idea that he started to publicly support it." It appears Galileo wrote about Copernican theory in Italian and Roman Catholic Church outpoured the curse upon him. A decree was passed against him.

All this couldn't hold Galileo who preferred to die in confinement than surrendering to the pressure and threats. Four years before his death in 1642, while he was still under house arrest, the manuscript of his book 'two new sciences' was smuggled to publishers in Holland. This got him the title of 'genius of modern physics'

Kepler, who also supported the Copernican theory, chose exile: "Hypocrisy I have never learned. I am in earnest about faith. I do not play with it."

This controversy is a brutal example of splitting a hair. This controversy is also based on the Aristotelian approach, 'Either this Or that'. Both the parties failed in understanding the 'genius of And' – this and that. Truth always remains a truth, only perception changes.

To my mind, allegory and metaphor are the way of expression in most of the scriptures. When Christ called God as 'My father' it was a metaphorical usage and not that he had claimed that he was born to God. One must read Bible carefully. Bible's usage of word 'father' at many places is in sense of 'God'. At numerous places even while addressing the mankind Bible uses the word, 'Your father'. One can't take the metaphorical usage literally. One may call mankind as 'children of God', that does not mean that all human beings are physically born to God. The usage of the word 'father' in Bible is metaphorical. If one reads those texts understanding the word 'father' metaphorically, one will conclude nothing but that this word stands for 'lord' or 'God'.

Metaphor...

If I say Hitler was a son of bitch, it doesn't mean that Hitler was born to a bitch. When I say, Mother Teresa was the holy angel, it only means that she was a holy person like an angel. But who can explain or convince those who are interested only in splitting the hair!

The controversy between the Catholic Church one hand and the cosmologists like Copernicus, Galileo and Kepler on the other, was the result of such 'splitting the hair', reading the biblical text too much between the lines least understanding its flavor of metaphor, allegory or parables.

It appears Galileo did argue that the Bible was not intended to tell us anything about scientific theories, and that it was usual to assume that where the Bible conflicted with common sense, it was being allegorical. But the Church did not give any heed to his arguments. Since Roman Catholic Church had declared 'Copernican theory' false, it was afraid of Protestants might make a scandal and get an edge. The feeling of inadequacy!

Now let me spin out the surprise that I promised at the beginning of this chapter...

Copernicus no doubt discovered first time what supposedly went against Biblical belief (I am not sure) and became the cause of collapsing the Aristotelian model. But as per today's knowledge I can say for sure, Copernicus was not all that right.

Let me begin first with his assumption that the Earth is orbiting around the Sun in a 'circular' orbit. Neither the Earth nor other planets are moving on a 'circular' orbit around the Sun. The orbit is elliptical, like an oval shape, and not 'circular' at the first place. Though Kepler supported 'Copernican theory', he modified it and suggested that the planets moved not in circles but in ellipses. This was confirmed and proved by Isaac Newton later. This discovery should comfort the Church that Copernicus was not all that right.

Now coming to another point of Copernican theory: that the Sun is stationary. Today it is proved that the Sun is not stationary.

I don't know why this point was not highlighted and Copernicus' view that 'Sun is stationary' not condemned by today's astronomers. Even the dare devil Stephan Hawking who takes a straight clash with the Church, undeterred of speaking truth as per his scientific discoveries is not found much vocal.

Today, the Sun is not stationary; the Sun was stationary a few decades ago, due to lack of our scientific knowledge.

Today it is discovered and proved by science that the Sun is not stationary. Like planets are orbiting around the Sun in a Solar System, the Sun is also moving in the Galaxy. This is a recent discovery – though discovered and published but not publicized. Why!

Why this fact that the Sun is also moving on its

orbit has been so much on 'low key'! This has been discovered and pronounced but almost in whispering tone. Since the purpose of my work is not to create controversy or bad blood, I am hesitant to ask the Western World, 'Is it because that this recent discovery confirms and conforms to the revelations of Qur'ãn?' Is 'West' afraid of Qur'ãnic Cosmology for Science is, today, going to be proved?

I would like to make loud and clear, what Holy Qur'ãn proclaimed fourteen hundred years back. It makes it clear the movement of the sun 'on its course', the fact that became known to us through science hardly a few decades back. First I will quote two verses from Surah Ya-sin and then substantiate it further with the proclamations made by Qur'ãn, not once but several times in several Surahs:

"And <u>the sun runs its course</u> for a period determined for it; that is the decree of (Him), the Exalted, Mighty and the All-knowing." (Yasin—36:38)

"It is not permitted to the sun to catch up the moon, nor can the Night outstrip the Day: Each (just) swims along in <u>(its own) orbit</u> (according to decree)."

(Yasin—36:40)

First I would quote Stephan Hawking: "A well known scientist (some say it was Bertrand Russell) once gave a public lecture on astronomy. He described how the Earth orbits around the Sun and how the Sun, in turn, orbits around centre of a vast collection of stars called galaxy..." This reveals that the not only the Earth orbits around the Sun but the Sun also orbits in the galaxy. The difference is only that the orbit of the Earth is Solar System and the orbit of the Sun is the galaxy.

Maurice Bucaille, who made an in-depth study of Qur'ãn gives his reasoning, "It is more difficult to conceive of the Sun's orbit because we are so used to seeing our solar system organized around it. To understand the verse from the Qur'ãn, the position of the Sun in our galaxy must be considered, and we must therefore call on modern scientific idea."

As I mentioned earlier, our galaxy, which is quite modest in size, consists of one hundred billion stars or planetary system. It is like a spiral disc. What we call 'Sun', like other stars, occupies a position in the galaxy. This position is far away from the point that constitutes the centre of the galaxy. Obviously, when the galaxy revolves on its axis, the sun would also revolve. It cannot afford to be stationary in a revolving galaxy. To understand this, one needs to change his 'frame of reference' from 'within solar system' to 'outside the solar system, but within the galaxy'. Had the sun been in the centre of the galaxy, it wouldn't be moving in the revolving galaxy. But the sun occupies a place, which is far away from the centre of the galaxy.

"The galaxy revolves on its own axis which is its centre with the result that the sun revolves around the same centre in a 'circular' orbit," writes Maurice in his 'The Bible, The Qur'ãn and Science'. "The modern astronomy has worked out the details of this. In 1917,

Shapley estimated the distance between the Sun and the centre of our galaxy as 10 kiloparsecs... To complete one revolution on its own axis, the galaxy and the sun take roughly 250 million years. The Sun travels at roughly 150 miles per second in the completion of this." To make the explanation simple, we can say that all the celestial bodies revolve around the centre on its axis.

"It is He who created the Night and the Day, and the sun and the moon: All (the celestial bodies) swim along, each in its round course." (Luqman—31:29)

"...That He has subjected the sun and the moon (to His laws), each running its course for a term appointed; and the Allah is well-acquainted with all that ye do?" (Luqman—31:29)

"And He hath made subject to you the sun and the moon, both diligently pursuing their courses..." (Ibrahim—14:33)

"He merges Night into Day, and He merges Day into Night, and He has subjected the sun and the moon (to His law): each one runs its course for a term appointed. Such is Allah your Lord, to Him belongs all domain. And those whom ye invoke besides Him have not the least power." (Fatir—35:13)

"... He has subjected the sun and the moon (to His law)! Each one runs (its course) for a term appointed. He doth regulate all affairs, explaining the Signs in details, that ye may believe with certainty in meeting with your Lord." (Ar-Rád—13:2)

To summarize:

- In the traditional model it was believed that it was the sun which was moving around the Earth and the Earth was stationary.
- Copernicus pressed his theory propounding that it was the Earth that moves around the Sun and the Sun was stationary.
- It recently came to light through science that though it is fact that the Earth moves around the Sun, but the Sun is not stationary. The Sun, like the Moon, or the Earth also moves on its course. The Sun is not motionless. It is also revolving along with the galaxy that is revolving.
- What made known to us by science just a few decades ago about the movement of the Sun (in the galaxy) was revealed to the humankind by the Holy Qur'ãn fourteen hundred years back.

I once again express my anguish on the approach of the astronomers who have not cared to go through the Qur'ãnic revelations especially the ones that pertain to cosmology. When scientists, astronomers, and physicists can make so much hue and cry on the controversy between the Catholic Church and the Copernican theory, how can they afford to keep silent when they discovered that the Sun is also revolving and moving on its course. Both, the Moon and the Sun orbit on their appointed courses. So clearly worded are the revelations of the Qur'ãn and no excitement has been shown either by Muslims who read Qur'ãn every day nor by the astronomers who preferred to remain ignorant of Qur'ãnic revelations. I invite them to read the above mentioned verses and proclaim that here is a Holy Scripture that revealed to humankind fourteen hundred years ago what that discovered just a few decades back by the scientists.

Perhaps this urge was beating in my heart that made me to have sleepless nights in reading and understanding Astronomy, a subject that was Latin and Greek to me until a couple of years back. Today I understand a grain of it.

The Sun is also moving on its course...

*****

'AS-SAA'

If the universe has come into being by Big Bang, it will disappear with Big Crunch is a scientific belief.

To quote from the Concise Columbia Encyclopedia, "The strongest evidence for the big bang theory is the feeble radio background radiation, discovered in 1960s, that is received from every part of sky. This radiation has a black-body temperature of 2.7 degrees above absolute zero and is interpreted as the electromagnetic remnants of the primordial fireball, stretched to long wave-length by the expansion of the universe."

According to another hypothesis, the steady-state theory, the universe expands, but new matter is continuously created at all points in space left by the receding galaxies; this theory now has few adherents.

It is Stephan Hawking who is working on the possibility that the cosmos will expand forever and not collapse in a big crunch as believed by most of the astronomers. Time has begun with big bang. If the universe goes on expanding, time will never end is his belief.

But we have discovered how perfect is the human knowledge about cosmos! Yesterday's knowledge is today's ignorance. Likewise today's understanding could be tomorrow's unawareness.

Almost all religions have expressed about doomsday. Everything that comes into existence shall vanish. The second law of thermodynamics, popularly known as entropy, precisely talks about such decadence.

As mentioned earlier, the big bang theory states that all of the matter and energy in the cosmos was concentrated in a very small volume that exploded between 10 and 20 billion years ago, and that the resulting expansion continues even today. Cosmos, large aggregation of gas, dust, and typically billions of stars, is held together by the gravitational attractions between its parts, and its rotational motion prevents it from collapsing on itself. In layman's language there are two forces working simultaneously – gravitational and repulsive. So long the repulsive force due to 'rotational' motion is stronger than the gravitational force, the universe will continue to expand.

Whether the universe's expansion will continue or eventually halt and reverse, with the Universe collapsing in the so-called big crunch remains unanswered by science. Most of the religions of the world refer to 'Doomsday' – the day of judgement. Does Doomsday direct to what the cosmologists call 'Big Crunch'?

The various Holy Scriptures are pregnant with oracles and suggestiveness. They do not directly and openly express or explain, but with their 'indicative meanings' they simply guide us to the very presence of Truth.

Big crunch is one of the scientific eventualities.

Time and space began with big bang and both will disappear with big crunch is the scientific belief. Today the cosmos is expanding, tomorrow the big crunch will suck it back – existence to non-existence. It happened to many stars in our galaxy and beyond our galaxy.

Big Crunch!

The Big Bang occurred with the ear deafening blast – the loudness of the blast was beyond measure. And those astronomers, cosmologists and physicists who talk today about Big Crunch, expect the same blast, the loudness beyond measure. Is it not a miracle that Holy Qur'ãn reveals unto us fourteen hundred years ago about the doomsday – the day of resurrection – with ear deafening blasting sound!

The Day when they will

Hear a (mighty) Blast

In (very) truth: that

Will be the Day

Of Resurrection (Qaf—50:42)

Sub'han Allah!

Holy Prophet says that the mystery will be made known only after 'as-saa' – the beginning of eternal life after the doomsday. "Things which no eye has seen, nor has ear heard, nor have they entered into the heart of men," (Bu. 59:8) will be made known, according to saying of the Holy Prophet. The very idea of time and space after 'as-saa' relating to the next world are different from those here.

In fact creation story of cosmos is a mystery; big bang is one such explanation. Even scientists stand divided when it comes to a final scientific conclusion. Holy Prophet says that the mystery will be known only after 'as-saa', the eternal life after this temporal life.

Carl Sagan, in his famous work 'Cosmos' writes about big bang with his shaky hand and mystified mind. "If the general picture of an expanding universe and a big bang is correct, we must then confront still more difficult questions. What were conditions like at the time of the big bang? What happened before that? Was there a tiny universe, devoid of all matter, and then the matter suddenly created from nothing? How does that happen? In many cultures it is customary to answer that God created the universe out of nothing... We must ofcourse ask next where God comes from. And if we decide this to be unanswerable, why not save a step and decide that the origin of the universe is an unanswerable question."

Before heaven and earth had taken form all was vague and amorphous... Creation story is a great mystery.

Stephan Hawking doesn't consider the creation story as mystery. But as he moves forward, he corrects what he thought correct earlier. Interesting!

In the article "Here for all eternity", Steve Connor writes, "With his new theory of what happened before the big bang, Stephan Hawking has changed the rules of time, suggesting the universe will expand forever... Hawking will, meanwhile, be working on rewording his chapter in 'A Brief History of Time' on the origin of universe to take his new theory into account." Does it mean that the 'theory of relativity' and singularity theory of big bang, what brought the pea-like early universe into existence with the divine spark, has now been ruled out by him?

Let us see what he claimed in his famous book 'A brief History of Time'. "The whole history of science has been the gradual realization that events do not happen in an arbitrary manner, but that they reflect a certain underlying order," asserts Stephan.

However he is not very sure whether the entire process was divinely inspired! At different place he expresses his views on big bang and big crunch. "According to the general theory of relativity, there must have been a state of infinite density in the past, the big bang, which would have been an effective beginning of time. Similarly, if the whole universe re-collapsed, there must be another state of infinite density in the future, the big crunch, which would be an end of time."

So the assumption is clear that both space and time will come to an end after the big crunch, what Qur'ãn says 'as-saa'.

Qur'ãn makes it clear that all that God has created will come to an end. The Last Day is an inescapable eventuality. Those who do not believe are not men of faith. "Truly, those who have faith (in this Qur'an), as well as those who follow the Jewish (faith), and the Christians and the Sabians – all who believe in God and the <u>Last Day,</u> and do righteous deeds, shall have their reward with their Sustainer: they need have no fear, neither shall they grieve."

(Al-Baqrah—2:62)

The creation of God was not for ever; it was for an appointed time. This has been revealed clearly in many surahs.

"...He has subjected the sun and the moon (to

His law) each one follows a course <u>for a time appointed</u>..." (Az-Zumar—39: 5)

"...He has subjected the sun and the moon (to His law)! Each one runs (its course) <u>for a term appointed</u>... (Ar-Rad—13:2)

"...That He has subjected the sun and the moon (to His laws), each running its course <u>for a term appointed</u>; and the Allah is well-acquainted with all that ye do?" (Luqman—31:29)

God has been quite unambiguous and stated His will in unclipped words that everything that He created and the processes that He set in motion is for an 'appointed time'. What is this appointed time is a mystery that remains unto Him. But he has indicated some manifestations in the Holy Qur'ãn:

"When the stars are made to disappear, and when the heaven is rent asunder, and when the mountains are carried away as dust, and when the apostles are made to reach their appointed time."

(Al-Mursalat—77:8-11)

"And when the trumpet is blown with a single blast, and the earth and the mountains, are borne away and crushed with a single crushing; on that day shall the great event come to pass..."

(Al-Haaqqa—69: 13-18)

Now let us take a scientific look about the future

of universe. The scientists are absolutely clear that science cannot predict the future. "In practice we cannot predict human behavior, even though we know the equations that govern it. Science cannot predict the future of human society or even if it has any future. The danger is that our power of damage or destroy the environment or one another is increasing much more rapidly than our wisdom in using this power," observes Stephan Hawking in his article 'The Future of the Universe'. If such wisdom-less progress continues, the scientists might bring the doomsday faster than fated, he means.

It is believed that the expansion of cosmos is quite smooth and not at all chaotic. Nonetheless, one would expect the gravitational attraction between different galaxies to be slowing down the rate of expansion. In simple words the gravitation force will become stronger than the repulsive force that is causing expansion. It is possible, believe some scientists. "If the density of the universe is greater than a certain 'critical value', gravitational attraction will eventually stop the expansion and make the universe start to contract again. The universe would collapse to a big crunch," could be one possibility as per Hawking's study. The big crunch again would be a singularity like big bang.

So, as per science the big crunch depends on

the question, 'What is the average density' in relation to the 'critical value'? If it is lesser than the 'critical value', what is known as Chandrasekhar limit, the universe will continue to expand. But if the density of cosmos were greater than the 'critical value' the big crunch would take place and the universe will re-collapse; time itself will come to an end. Hawking holds that the known density of cosmos is not even 1% of the critical value. But what is unknown to scientists is the real mass of the black holes, which could be in terms of many galaxies.

'Black holes' exist and scientists as well as cosmologists recognise them. What is black hole? In layman's language it is the collapse of star when its average mass become lesser than the 'critical value' – the gravitational force overpowers the repulsive force and causes the collapse. It is so simple to understand. It is nothing but a big crunch for an individual star, when it goes into black hole. So the big crunch could be for a singular star, it could be for a galaxy, and the ultimate big crunch what we have been discussing could be in terms of universes or cosmos. To sum up, the eventuality of big crunch in relation to stars and galaxies is a scientific knowledge. What remains unknown to science in relation to entire universe or cosmos. The debate is not on collapse, the debate is on the size of collapse. For humankind the collapse of our planet on which we live is eventually the big crunch for no one would live to know about rest of the heavenly bodies. With this idealized test, I conclude that doomsday is fated even scientifically and the humankind cannot escape.

To quote a few more Verses from Qur'ãn about the doomsday:

"...When the sight becomes confused, and the moon becomes dark, and the sun and the moon are brought together. Man shall say on that day, whither to flee to?..." (Al-Qiyamat—75:7-10)

"...the hour (as-saa) is their promised time and the hour shall most grievous and bitter." (Al-Qamer—54:46)

"when the earth shall be changed into a different earth and the heavens as well" (Ibrahim—14:48)

Einstein's general theory of relativity makes clear and predicts that space-time that began at the big bang singularity would come to an end either at the big crunch singularity, if the whole universe re-collapsed, or at the singularity inside a black hole, if a local region, such as a star, were to collapse. In either of the two cases, the impact on humankind is the same so long the star or the planet happens to be mother earth – the only planet where life exists as per today's knowledge. Life will come to end with collapse of the solar system, or the galaxy or the universe or one of them.

'As-Saa' is the pre-determined eventuality.

*****

About Moid Siddiqui

Moid Siddiqui is a New Age corporate professional with a bandwidth of interests and expertise ranging form Human Potential Development to producing Mnagement Films. He has served the industry in senior capacities including board level positions in several premier public and private sector organizations in India, viz. BHEL, NHPC, CCI, HMT, BEML, Nagarjuna Group. Presently he is working as Professor in Centre for Organization Development sharing with others what he has learned as a corporate practitioner for the past three decades. He is a unique blend of a practitioner and educator.

Moid Siddiqui is a strong believer in 'Intangibles' and 'Softer' side of Management, what he calls his passion – Managing through Sense and Soul. He has authored four management books, namely, 'The Brave New Manager', 'Management Parables' 'Intangibles – the obverse phase of management', and 'Honk – Learn from Animal Kingdom'. Tata Mac-Graw Hill published the first book. Prism Books Pvt. Ltd. published the other three books. His fifth book, 'Heartware – The Art of Managing from Within' is being reviewed by

Sage Publishers. His sixth book, 'Ancient Wisdom for New Age' is under review by John Wiley, Singapore.

His articles were published in American Society for Training & Development's professional journal 'Training and Development'. Through his articles, books and thoughts, he has challenged the conventional approach and pointed towards the direction of wholeness through intuitive wisdom. He is known for his innovative pattern of language.

Moid Siddiqui is the recipient of several honours and awards including the All India Management Association's Best Management Book of 1996 for 'The Brave New Manager', The International Greenland Society Gold Award and The Rajiv Gandhi Memorial National Award. He has also scripted and directed several management videos on productivity, organizational development and industrial relations. Door Darshan telecast his film 'Shraddhanjahali', on national network; Late Mr. Rajiv Gandhi, the then Prime Minister of India wrote a letter of appreciation to him.

Moid Siddiqui has carried out a research study on 'Performance Management System' at International Resource Centre, UK and participated in the Global Convention organized by State of the World Forum at San Francisco, California in October, 1999 on the theme 'Envisioning and Creating a Sustainable

Compassionate Society' – a step towards creating a culture of peace.

Moid Siddiqui scripted/produced three Management Video Films:

- The Pathway to Excellence – a Management 'Film on PIP
- The Art of Negotiation (Script)
- Where Do We Go From Here? (For OD Interventions)

Moid Siddiqui's current interests are spirituality and cosmology. His inquisitive mind keeps him vibrant and thinking. "It is easy to utter 'Allah-u-Akbar", says Moid. "But unless we understand a bit about the Earth, Solar System, our galaxy (Milky Way) and Cosmos we cannot fathom the extent of greatness of Allah." This thought was the turning point which made him to make an in-depth study of cosmology.

You may reach to Moid Siddiqui thro email: moidsiddiqui@yahoo.com, or sms: +919848049944

***